# It's Easy To
# Jazz Guitar

## by Joe Bennett

**Wise Publications**
London / New York / Paris / Sydney / Copenhagen / Madrid / Tokyo

Exclusive Distributors:
Music Sales Limited
8/9 Frith Street, London W1D 3JB, England.
Music Sales Corporation
257 Park Avenue South, New York, NY10010, USA.
Music Sales Pty Limited
120 Rothschild Avenue, Rosebery, NSW 2018, Australia.

Order No. AM955185
ISBN 0-7119-8009-8
This book © Copyright 2000 Wise Publications

Written by Joe Bennett.
Edited by Sorcha Armstrong.
Musical examples by Richard Barrett.
Music processed by Digital Music Art.
Additional research by Jill Warren.
Jazz Family Tree by Cliff Douse.
Thanks to Kit Morgan, Mark Anderson, Andy Keep.

Book design by Phil Gambrill.
Cover design by Michael Bell Design.
Illustrations by Andy Hammond.

Text photographs courtesy of London Features International, except:
Joe Pass (page 22); John McLaughlin (page 24);
George Benson and Al Di Meola (page 28);
Stanley Jordan (page 29) - Redferns.
Picture of Lenny Breau (page 27) courtsey of String Jazz/ Stephen D. Anderson.

Printed in the United Kingdom by
Printwise (Haverhill) Limited, Haverhill, Suffolk.

Your Guarantee of Quality:
As publishers, we strive to produce
every book to the highest commercial standards.
The music has been freshly engraved and the book has
been carefully designed to minimise awkward page turns
and to make playing from it a real pleasure.
Particular care has been given to specifying acid-free,
neutral-sized paper made from pulps which have not
been elemental chlorine bleached.
This pulp is from farmed sustainable forests and
was produced with special regard for the environment.
Throughout, the printing and binding have been
planned to ensure a sturdy, attractive publication
which should give years of enjoyment.
If your copy fails to meet our high standards, please
inform us and we will gladly replace it.

Music Sales' complete catalogue describes thousands
of titles and is available in full colour sections by subject,
direct from Music Sales Limited.
Please state your areas of interest and send
a cheque/postal order for £1.50 for postage to: Music Sales Limited,
Newmarket Road, Bury St. Edmunds, Suffolk IP33 3YB.

www.musicsales.com

The one and only **Django Reinhardt** – possibly the best-loved

# Introduction

'Jazz' is probably the most inaccurately-used term in guitar music. Blues-rock bands will play a straight 12-bar, replace all the power chords with 7ths, and call it 'jazzy'. Dance acts will use a sample of a guitarist playing a minor 9th chord and call it 'acid-jazz-fusion-hiphop'. Heavy metal players will learn the Dorian mode from a scale book, play it up and down at 250 beats per minute, and then ramble on about the influence of jazz on their style.

Unfortunately, a great deal of true jazz guitar playing takes years - sometimes decades - of practice. To become truly proficient, you may have to learn (ugh!) scales and (yuk!) arpeggios and possibly even (aaaaargh!) to read music. Luckily, help is at hand.

*It's Easy To Bluff...Jazz Guitar* explains how, with the right information, equipment, name-dropping skills and attitude, you can become an expert in all the local customs of 'planet jazz'. Learn what to say and when to say it. Find out which players you can mention at a gig without ridicule. And play solos that will have other musicians worshipping at your feet.

# For Example

Guitarists naturally have a tendency to judge each other by technical skill. The jazz bluffer need show no fear, even when confronted with the most well-practised virtuoso. Any rival who can play stunning arpeggios at 10 notes per second can be dismissed as 'passé', 'retro', or 'just too clinical'.

Players who achieve super-accurate scalic runs should be accused of 'having no feel' or 'missing the point'. Of course, if you get stuck in a situation when your playing really is on the line, we've helpfully supplied just a smattering of impressive musical examples which you can throw into solos whenever you think the audience need reminding of your complete mastery of the instrument.

*It's Easy To Bluff... Jazz Guitar* gives you an unfair advantage over other guitarists. It's an immoral, cheating, deceitful, unethical and deceptive way of improving your guitar playing. But it will put you one step ahead of the next bluffer. Remember, as a wise Chicago jazzer once said –
"If you're being chased by a guy with a knife, you don't need to run faster than him, man. You just need to outrun your buddies..."

# The History Of Jazz or 'How To Start A Fight In A Jazz Club'

If you're going to get maximum credibility among the jazz fraternity, you've got to know your history. And the trick when bluffing your way through a jazz history conversation is always to go back earlier than anyone else. Someone likes George Benson? Tell them they should check out Wes Montgomery – he was George's biggest influence. They already know everything about Wes? Get in there quick with a reference to Charlie Christian – Montgomery's first job involved copying Christian's solos note-for-note. You get the idea.

## The Early Years

Leadbelly

So it stands to reason that if you're going to predate everyone else's references, you've got to start pretty early – before jazz began, in fact. In the early 1900s the only form of popular guitar music was the blues. Guitar players would add solo lines in between vocal phrases, and these improvised ideas eventually led to the development of jazz lead playing.

Now with this stuff, of course, you can bluff all you like about the music, because no recordings exist, and no-one wrote down any of the material as sheet music. If you do want to beef up your credibility in the CD department, get some remastered recordings by early bluesmen such as **Leadbelly**, **Big Bill Broonzy**, and **Blind Lemon Jefferson**.

The first 'jazz' guitar players came from New Orleans marching bands, and the earliest known one of these was **Buddy Bolden**'s Jazz Band. In 1895 they were photographed with guitar player Brock Mumford. Again, we don't know what Brock sounded like, but we can be pretty sure he was a rhythm guitar man. The simple reason for this is that the guitar wasn't amplified, and he was up against two clarinets, a cornet and a trombone.

# Electricity!

**During the 1920s the two most important events in jazz guitar history occurred – the Western Electric recording process, and the earliest guitar solos.**

Lonnie Johnson

One of the earliest jazzers to make use of both was the black blues singer and guitarist **Lonnie Johnson**. As well as recording under his own name as early as 1925, he sat in on sessions for jazz greats such as **Duke Ellington** and **Louis Armstrong**.

Shortly afterwards, virtuoso jazz soloist **Eddie Lang** appeared on the scene. The two were soon dueting together, although Lang had to use a pseudonym – he was a white player, and the US wasn't quite ready yet for black and white musicians to be seen collaborating.

# Charlie and Django

**Some great guitar players appeared in the USA during the 1930s, mainly as part of the rhythm section for the big band craze – George Van Eps, Dick McDonough and Teddy Bunn are just three of the many underrated chordal players from this era.**

However, two names dominated early electric guitar soloing during the late 1930s. **Charlie Christian** and **Django Reinhardt** are so famous amongst jazz bluffers that they are the only players to be referred to by first names only.

 # History Hint

The 'done thing' in conversations about **Django** is to say the name quietly but with a hint of affection – sort of giving the impression that you're on his wavelength. It's a bit tougher to do this with **Charlie Christian**, because people think you're referring to the equally bluffed-about sax player **Charlie Parker**.

# Bebop and Bossa

Charlie Christian & Gene Krupa

In the 1940s, along with the rest of the jazz scene, guitarists began experimenting with more complex chords, melodic lines and structures. The death of large, expensive bands led to a new type of jazz, referred to as bop, or bebop.

Virtuosos like **Barney Kessel** and **Tal Farlow** did for the guitar what **Charlie Parker** and **Dizzy Gillespie** were doing for sax and trumpet. Wild harmonies, crazy solos and outrageous speed set Bebop apart from the laid-back perfection of swing.

By now the electric guitar had become accepted as a serious solo instrument. Gibson's ES-150, popularised by **Charlie** (**Christian**!) came out in 1935, and spawned dozens of other semi-acoustic models. Throughout the 1940s (and for many players, ever since), Gibson f-hole guitars were *the* jazz instrument to own.

# Hard Bop and Cool

Soon, some of these jazz cats decided to take things a little slower, and the style evolved into 'Cool', which lasted well into the 1960s. Bop resurfaced in the late '50s when a bunch of caffeine-fuelled virtuosos took up hard bop – basically the result of trying to play very fast indeed over the top of an extremely loud Hammond Organ.

Wes Montgomery

Names to drop from the period include **Wes Montgomery**, **Kenny Burrell**, **Johnny Smith**. For extra bluff points, mention **Grant Green**. He wasn't the most famous of these, but he's guaranteed to give you instant cred (having died prematurely from a drug-related illness and also being highly underrated by many guitarists).

# The 70s — Are You Ready To Rock?!

**Although laid-back, subtle-sounding hollow-body guitar players were still recording at this time (Wes Montgomery, Joe Pass, and a young George Benson), the influence of loud amps, the fuzzbox, and solid-bodied guitars was unavoidable. In the late '60s Larry Coryell and John McLaughlin were pioneers of the style that became known as Fusion, or jazz-rock.**

Fusion continued throughout the 1970s, and technique was the name of the game. Virtuosos such as **Pat Metheny**, **McLaughlin** and **John Scofield** experimented more with amps and effects, and soon their rock-influenced solos started to include even more bizarre harmonies and scales. This superfast 'second wave' of guitar Fusion is frowned upon by some players these days (including **Scofield** and **John Abercrombie**, who pioneered it) but you have to hand it to those guys – this stuff was tough!

# Meanwhile, by the campfire...

**Acoustic guitarists were burning up the fingerboard too. Al Di Meola followed Larry Coryell in the Guitar Trio with McLaughlin and flamenco player Paco De Lucia.**

**Earl Klugh** and **George Benson** recorded acoustics together. By the 1980s, virtuosos such as **Martin Taylor**, **Tuck Andress** and **Michael Hedges** were creating incredible solo arrangements, and technique with taste was the order of the day.

# Jazz is Dead?

**Some will tell you that the golden age of jazz guitar has been and gone. Take them outside and give them a good... bluffing.**

The scene has never been so healthy. Admittedly, lots of material shows classic influences – **Wes** and **Django** particularly can still be heard in many contemporary players' albums – but there are still some great new players around. You can be sure that in 100 years' time, players such as **Ron Affif**, **Wayne Krantz** and **Mark Whitfield** will all be appearing in *It's Easy To Bluff... 21st Century Jazz Guitar*.

# Jazz Timeline

### 1890s

Ragtime and early jazz bands. But you couldn't hear the guitar.

### 1910s

Jazz begins in New Orleans...

### 1930s

The Swing era. Big bands kept guitar players in work. Amplification arrives and they start to take solos. **Django** appears on the scene. Start of **Charlie Christian**'s very short career.

### 1950s

Hard Bop and Cool jazz appear. Death of **Django**. Classical guitars used for jazz (**Laurindo Almeida, Charlie Byrd**).

### 1970s

Fusion continues and becomes even more jazzy. Mahavishnu Orchestra formed. Use of fuzzboxes really starts to get out of hand. Everyone wants to sound like the violin player. Acoustic guitar jazz groups spring up.

### 1990+

Anything goes! Lots of 'back to roots' stuff; **Scofield** goes acoustic, so does **Holdsworth. McLaughlin** back to Indian fusion with **Remember Shakti**. Guitar synthesisers sensibly abandoned by most. Name check: **Tribal Tech/ Scott Henderson, Wayne Krantz**.

### 1890-1910

Blues develops in Mississippi – solo singer with guitar and a chip on his shoulder.

### 1900s

Ragtime & blues start the roots of jazz. The guitarists are still pretty quiet.

### 1920s

...and becomes popular all over USA. **Leadbelly, Eddie Lang** and **Lonnie Johnson** are your main bluffs here.

### 1940s

The end of Swing and the start of Bebop (**Barney Kessell, Tal Farlow**). **Django** still on the scene. Electric solid-bodies start to appear. Everyone wants to sound like the saxophone player.

### 1960s

**Wes Montgomery** makes it big, but for a while Jazz takes second place to rock and fusion is born. Jazz guitar courses start in the USA. Fuzzboxes begin to frighten the old school and inspire the youngsters. Name-check **John McLaughlin** and **Larry Coryell** (fusion) or **George Benson**.

### 1980s

The decade of the shredders. **Allan Holdsworth, Frank Gambale, Frank Zappa** and **Steve Vai** all take up various positions in the middle ground between rock and jazz. At the other end of the scale, **Pat Metheny, Bill Frisell** and **George Benson** keep things melodic and mellow. Guitar synthesisers used by some.

# It's Easy To Bluff... Influences

If you get really stuck, use our handy Bluffer's Jazz Family Tree shown on this page. Remember, if someone gets clever about one player, just move one branch up the tree and outbluff them...

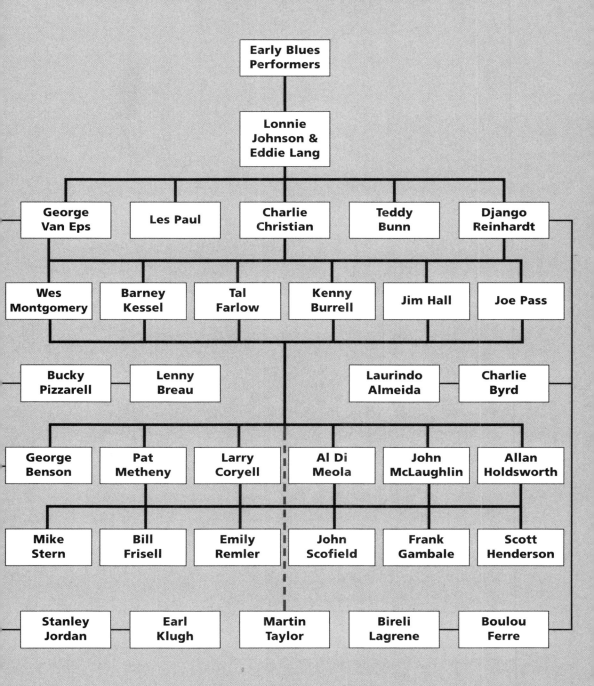

**Wes Montgomery** - one of the greats, but he couldn't read a chord chart!

# The Players

## Bite-size biogs

In this section you'll find an instant guide to six top jazz guitarists. Remember that these aren't necessarily the most 'important' players, but they are the most 'significant' (i.e. these are the ones to mention if you want to impress people!).

For each artist, I've included some basic **biography information**, notes on **playing style**, plus (more importantly) which **techniques** you should steal in order to facilitate your jazz career. Of course, you have to know the guitar they used - equipment trainspotters are everywhere and could pounce at any time.

To save you from having to wade through a truckload of CDs, I've also picked out one **essential album** for you to mention (not necessarily the best-known - it can sometimes pay dividends to bluff your way by showing you listen to the obscure stuff). If you're actually asked to prove that you've heard the artist, you'd be stuck without the quick and easy '**finest moment**' reference, and you'll find it helpful to casually mention your handy '**knowledgeable fact**'.

Finally, it's always useful to have a few oven-ready opinions up your sleeve. For each player, I've included an 'instant opinion' (usually ambiguous enough to cover all situations) and an 'acceptable criticism'. If you're cool enough to criticise one of the greats, you can consider your status as a true jazzer to be totally foolproof.

## Bluffing Tip

It's highly advisable to try to hear at least a couple of tracks by each of these guys. The last thing you want to hear when discussing a player you've never heard is the dreaded words "So what's your favourite track?".

# Lonnie Johnson 1894-1970

**ORIGIN:**
New Orleans, USA

**STYLE:**
Blues-jazz

**HISTORY AND BACKGROUND:**
First recorded under his own name as a guitarist as early as 1925 ('**Mr Johnson's Blues**'). Still thought of by many as a blues artist, but his solo guitar lines are undeniably jazzy. Guested with **Louis Armstrong**'s Hot Five in the late '20s, before moving upmarket to the (larger) **Duke Ellington** orchestra. Signed with Okeh Records in 1925, and proceeded to make an estimated 130 recordings during the next 7 years. Between 1928 and 1929 he recorded some white-hot duets with **Eddie Lang** (who was using the pseudonym **Blind Willie Dunn**). Pioneered 12-string as a solo jazz instrument (while Leadbelly did the same for the instrument in Country-Blues).

Career took a dip in the 1950s (Johnson worked as a janitor), until he had renewed success on the touring and festivals circuit in the 1960s. One of the earliest guitar heroes in jazz history, and massively influential on everyone from **Robert Johnson** to **Elvis Presley** and **Jerry Lee Lewis**, who both paid tribute by recording versions of his hit 'Tomorrow Night'.

**PLAYING STYLE:**
Forceful flatpicked single-note solos, with loads of freedom and flexibility in the timing.

### TECHNIQUES TO STEAL:

Picking solos on an acoustic 12-string *very hard indeed*. This was the 1920s, remember, and someone had yet to put a pickup on a guitar.

### GEAR:

Grunewald 12-string, Gibson J100. Later, Kay solid-body and Martin acoustic.

### BLUFFER'S ALBUM:

Check out the **Eddie Lang** compilation album *Jazz Guitar Virtuoso*, which includes the legendary duets he recorded with Johnson. For solo stuff, get *Steppin' On The Blues*, his first (and most ground-breaking) album.

### FINEST MOMENT:

His duets with **Lang** contain some of his most accomplished and inspired playing, but his biggest hit was the mellow ballad 'Tomorrow Night', which topped the R&B charts for seven weeks in 1948.

### KNOWLEDGEABLE FACT:

Originally started out as a violin player (as did **Eddie Lang**).

### INSTANT OPINION:

Blues guitar (and therefore Jazz) simply would not have developed in the way that it did without **Lonnie Johnson**.

### ACCEPTABLE CRITICISM:

Picked up an electric in the mid-1940s, with less success.

# Django Reinhardt 1910-1953

**ORIGIN:**
Belgian-Gypsy

**STYLE:**
Swing

**HISTORY AND BACKGROUND:**
Django was born into a gypsy family – his father worked as a travelling show entertainer. Originally learned banjo and violin. A caravan fire in 1928 damaged his hand, and while he recovered, his gypsy friends loaned him a guitar. His third and fourth fingers were locked at the first joint due to the fire, so he could use them for basic chord shapes only – he then developed the two-finger lead style which was his trademark.

The famous Quintet du Hot Club de France was formed in 1934 and featured Django and violinist **Stephane Grappelli** as part of a line-up of three guitars, bass and fiddle. **The Quintet** had international success until 1939. Django travelled Europe and the USA throughout the war, settling down in the late 1940s to record his biggest hit 'Nuages'. Died in 1953, having suffered a brain haemorrhage.

**PLAYING STYLE:**
High-speed (acoustic) single-note runs and arpeggios (with or without bends), punctuated with partial chord stabs.

## TECHNIQUES TO STEAL:

Set up a swing groove at a high tempo ($\quarternote$=200+) and play arpeggiated swung quavers over it – if you can!

## GEAR:

Selmer-Macaferri acoustic with characteristic 'D' shaped soundhole, although he also played a borrowed archtop f-hole acoustic for one post-war tour. Added a pickup to the Macaferri later, and went fully electric in 1950.

## ESSENTIAL ALBUM:

Any Quintet du Hot Club de France compilation is essential listening. For maximum cred, try some of his really late recordings (early 1950s) – he's just starting to get into bop.

## FINEST MOMENT:

You should learn 'Nuages' note-for-note anyway because it's such a technique-fest. Many players feel he's at his best when performing standards, adding fun and astonishing ideas to established classics. Check out his versions of 'Sweet Georgia Brown' and 'Ain't Misbehavin'.

## KNOWLEDGEABLE FACT:

Although he's best-known for the European Hot Club material, Django also worked with big American names such as **Duke Ellington**, **Glenn Miller** and **Dizzy Gillespie** during the 1940s.

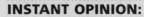

## INSTANT OPINION:

"Reinvented jazz for Europe".

## ACCEPTABLE CRITICISM:

Bien sûr, you are joking, n'est pas?

# Charlie Christian 1916-1942

**ORIGIN:**
Texas/Oklahoma, USA

**STYLE:**
Swing and Bop

**HISTORY AND BACKGROUND:**
Jazz guitar was literally in the background. Then Charlie plugged in, and everyone could hear what was going on. Although a fine player, his most significant contribution to jazz is that he turned the guitar almost overnight into a big-band instrument that could take solos. During his early career in the 1930s he began experimenting with ways of making the guitar louder, including miking up the soundhole or even trying to play with a microphone inside the body. The Gibson company perfected the process of combining an f-hole archtop with a pickup in 1936, and Charlie's vision of a single-note electric guitar solo could be realised.

Although he wasn't the first to use an electric guitar (**Eddie Durham** used a home-made one as early as 1935), his sax-style solos were the first to make it popular (he was clearly influenced by saxophonist **Lester Young**). He recorded for less than two years, with **Benny Goodman**, **Count Basie** and **Dizzy Gillespie**, and died of tuberculosis (combined with a rather extreme jazz lifestyle) in 1942.

**PLAYING STYLE:**
Single-note solos, heavily based around the arpeggios, played more delicately than his all-acoustic predecessors. Warm, middly tone.

## TECHNIQUES TO STEAL:
Play extended arpeggios that take the chord backing further
(e.g. if you're hearing a chord of C, play B, D and F to imply Cmaj11).
Then experiment with the timing of these so you're slightly behind or
ahead of the beat. Hmmm... yes, it *is* easier said than done, isn't it?

## GEAR:

The Gibson ES-150 (the first production electric
archtop) quickly became known as the **Charlie
Christian** model.

## ESSENTIAL ALBUM:
Get the compilation *The Genius of the Electric Guitar* (or any compilation
which includes his **Goodman** recordings) – that's all you'll need.

## FINEST MOMENT:
'Solo Flight' with Goodman is, er, good, man. His beautiful
version of the standard 'Stardust' is another stand-out.

## KNOWLEDGEABLE FACT:
After an unsuccessful initial meeting, Charlie got the
job with **Benny Goodman** by getting jazz promoter **John
Hammond** to set up his guitar on stage for him while the band were
taking a break. When the band got back, Charlie was sitting there
waiting to play. **Benny** didn't want to make a fuss in a fairly tough venue,
so went along with it. Charlie's solos turned a 3-minute tune into a
45-minute improvisation. He was hired.

## INSTANT OPINION:
**"Without Charlie Christian, the electric guitar just
wouldn't have sounded the same. Without the
electric guitar, Charlie Christian just wouldn't
have sounded the same."**

## ACCEPTABLE CRITICISM:
His playing is often so *right* that he could be accused of being 'safe'.
But make sure you can play all of his licks before you start to criticise
them in company...

# Wes Montgomery 1925-1968

**ORIGIN:**
Indiana, USA

**STYLE:**
Cool

**HISTORY AND BACKGROUND:**
Wes had success fairly late in life. He got his first guitar aged ten, and bought an electric when he was 18. But until the age of 34 he held down regular day jobs, including factory work, with a semi-pro gigging career in the evenings. He was a completely self-taught player – allegedly he couldn't even read a chord sheet – so his natural skill on the instrument was entirely a result of hard work combined with a phenomenal musical ear.

His debut, *Introducing Wes Montgomery*, was recorded in 1959, and he became an instant success on the Cool jazz scene. During the late 1960s he recorded various albums of standards or even straight-ahead pop covers, showing a commercialism that's easy criticism material for the novice bluffer. He died in 1968 of a heart attack.

**PLAYING STYLE:**
Two words – octave and thumb. Wes devised his own fingerings for parallel octaves, and developed incredible skill at switching shapes at speed. He also played using thumb downstrokes, apparently to avoid upsetting the neighbours while practising.

### TECHNIQUES TO STEAL:

Try playing a simple tune on one string. Now try fretting the octave version of it (on the next string but one). Now slide the shape up and down, muting the string in between with the side of the finger, keeping the shape intact throughout. That's your basic octave technique. Use a warm, middly guitar tone and (fairly hard) downstrokes with the thumb. After playing a few solos this way, break into regular single-note picking for a while, then go back to the octaves. Classic Wes.

### GEAR:

Gibson L5CES f-hole big-bodied archtop with twin humbuckers.

### ESSENTIAL ALBUM:

There are two you should own. *The Incredible Jazz Guitar of Wes Montgomery* is perhaps the most exciting, but the live recording *Smokin' At The Half Note* is also essential.

### FINEST MOMENT:

His version of 'Gone With The Wind' has got it all. It starts with single-note lines, shifts unexpectedly into octaves, and then goes into the theme played in chords (bluffer's tip – when you hear this bit, smile knowingly and say "Ah, you see, that's where he's doing a **Barney Kessel**").

### KNOWLEDGEABLE FACT:

Got his first gig copying **Charlie Christian** solos note-for-note.

### INSTANT OPINION:

"He was discovered too late and died too soon."

### ACCEPTABLE CRITICISM:

Style hardly developed during his career.

# Joe Pass 1929-1994

**ORIGIN:**
New Jersey/Pennsylvania, USA

**STYLE:**
Bop, but tried pretty much everything except Fusion. Famous for unaccompanied arrangements of standards.

**HISTORY AND BACKGROUND:**
Original name **Joseph Anthony Jacobi Passalaqua**. He was a completely self-taught player with a natural gift for (re-) harmonising tunes. Started to get interested in Bop in the 1940s, but soon developed the drug problem often associated with the style. Found himself institutionalised in 1960 in the Synanon Foundation's rehab centre. His first album was a compilation of patients' work called *Sounds of Synanon*.

Sensibly recorded a **Django** tribute album in 1964 (a classic bluffer's trick which rarely fails) and the now-revered album *Simplicity* in 1966. Hooked up with guitarist **Herb Ellis** in 1971 and formed yet another of jazz guitar's cherished duos, then moved on to join piano player **Oscar Peterson**. In 1973 he recorded *Virtuoso*, a collection of unaccompanied tunes which defined his style as a solo player.

Continued to work with big guitar names right up until his death, including **John Williams**, **John Pisano** and **Paco Peña**.

### PLAYING STYLE:

Clean sound, combining bassline, chords and melody. Sometimes fast arpeggiated runs which imply complex backing chords.

### TECHNIQUES TO STEAL:

If you can steal **Joe Pass'** technique, you should be writing this book, not reading it.

### GEAR:

Gibson ES175; Ibanez signature model; D'Aquisto.

### ESSENTIAL ALBUM:

No question – the *Virtuoso* series of albums (now available as a set on CD).

### FINEST MOMENT:

For technique, probably his solo version of the Bop standard 'Cherokee'. For sheer beautiful guitar playing, get the Joe Pass/Ella Fitzgerald album *Take Love Easy*.

### KNOWLEDGEABLE FACT:

When Joe adapted his technique to incorporate fingerstyle so he could play solo arrangements, he complained that the lack of a plectrum slowed him down. No-one else had noticed.

### INSTANT OPINION:

"He had a natural feel for changes, not just playing over them but adding to them."

### ACCEPTABLE CRITICISM:

Never experimented with effects, believing that all emotions could be portrayed with a clean sound.

# John McLaughlin b.1942

**ORIGIN:**
Yorkshire, UK

**STYLE:**
Fusion/World

**HISTORY AND BACKGROUND:**
Grew up in a (classical) musical family and was a working rock & pop session player by his early 20s. Studied the music of all the jazz greats throughout, and was soon discovered by **Miles Davis**, with whom he made two early albums. Recorded early fusion albums as a solo artist or in bands, until 1970, when he met his spiritual guru **Sri Chinmoy**. Formed **The Mahavishnu Orchestra**, which was possibly the biggest influence on jazz and jazz-rock in the 1970s.

From mid-70s onwards he went in various directions – an all-acoustic trio (with **Al Di Meola** and **Paco do Lucia**); **Shakti**, an Indian music/jazz improv project; plus various orchestral ventures. During 1999, he had two projects on the go - *Remember Shakti* (title of 1999 Indian-influenced album) and **Heart of Things,** a gigging Fusion band.

**PLAYING STYLE:**
Very fast indeed. Lots of repeated picked figures that often *sound* like simple pentatonics, but have subtle extra jazz notes added to demonstrate that John is a student of The School Of Extreme Cleverness.

## TECHNIQUES TO STEAL:

There are two unusual techniques you should try. Firstly, don't use *any* hammer-ons or pull-offs – every note should be individually picked, however fast the tempo. Secondly, start every picked phrase on a plectrum *upstroke*. Once you can do this, try it using the Lydian ♭7 mode with chromatic links at 250 BPM. Playing semiquaver triplets. In 13/8 time.

## GEAR:

Bogue double-neck; Les Paul; ES345; Gibson J200 custom acoustic with DeArmond pickup; Gibson SG-style double-neck 6/12; Wechter 'Shakti' guitar with scalloped neck and sympathetic drone strings across the soundhole.

## ESSENTIAL ALBUM:

*My Goals Beyond* (1971) was the album that resurrected the acoustic guitar in jazz at the time. It came between his early fusion days and the start of **Mahavishnu**. Alternatively, any early **Mahavishnu** album in the rack really shows that you know not only your jazz but your World music – two bluffs for the price of one!

## FINEST MOMENT:

Check out 'The Life Divine' from the album *Love, Devotion and Surrender* which he recorded with **Carlos Santana**.

## KNOWLEDGEABLE FACT:

In the 1960s, **Johnny McLaughlin** (as he was then) played with the Top Of The Pops band, **Tom Jones**, and **Dusty Springfield**. He appeared on the first **Bowie** album, and even played sessions with the **Rolling Stones**.

## INSTANT OPINION:

"Can play any kind of music with anyone."

## ACCEPTABLE CRITICISM:

Notoriously difficult to work with.

# Emergency Backup Bluffs

In these pages you'll find condensed factfiles on a further 10 players. These aren't meant to be comprehensive, but they should give you enough information to get by in most situations.

## 1. Eddie Lang (1902-33)

Born **Salvatore Massaro**, and occasionally used the pseudonym **Blind Willie Dunn**. Played Gibson L4/L5 archtops and Martin D42 acoustic. Established an international reputation playing solo, then went on to duet famously with **Lonnie Johnson** and violinist **Joe Venuti**. Single-string picking technique and acute chord patterns set the standards for early jazz guitar. He went on to develop 'chamber jazz', placing virtuoso improvisation in a controlled setting - check out his version of 'Tiger Rag'. In early 1930s worked as accompanist to smoothie **Bing Crosby**.

## 2. Charlie Byrd (1925-2000)

Classical guitar with jazz technique. Famed for his versatility, using Ramirez and Ovation Spanish nylon-strung guitars. Dispensed with the plectrum to perfect a sleepy Samba sound and was fond of combining cool Bossa Nova with classical solos. Collaborated with the Brazilian masters **Jobim** and **Gilberto**. 1974 recording of 'Great Guitars' was made with **Kessel** and **Herb Ellis**. Generally regarded as easy to listen to but almost impossible to copy.

# 3. Barney Kessel (b.1923)

Well-loved jazz guitarist, famed for his liquid chord style. Played Gibson ES350 and his own Gibson signature model. Starred in bands led by **Oscar Peterson**, **Artie Shaw** and **Chico Marx**. Accompanied major female vocalists like **Ella Fitzgerald** and **Sarah Vaughan**, and played on **Julie London**'s classic 'Cry Me a River'.

Was generally happiest when playing solo - even sessions for **The Beach Boys** and **Phil Spector** did not cheer him up. Suffered a stroke in 1992, but got tentatively back into the guitar in the late 90s.

# 4. Lenny Breau (1941-1984)

Another seven-string disciple, eventually designing his own model using an extra treble string, later produced by Sand and Dauphin.

Known as 'the guitarist's guitarist', influenced originally by **Chet Atkins**. Despite drug addiction and spells of illness he recorded some fine work - e.g. *Velvet Touch Of Lenny Breau*.

Gave live master classes in his fingerstyle approach. Shame that most people only know of him because he was found murdered in a swimming pool in 1984.

# 5. George Benson (b.1943)

Jazz/funk/soul guitarist and vocalist. Plays a Gibson Super 400CES and his own Ibanez signature model. Transcended the jazz-funk divide to become a key player in the A&M stable when chosen to follow in the wake of **Wes Montgomery**.

Particularly skilled in improvising guitar lines in unison with own scat singing – this style is still referred to as 'doing a George Benson'. 1976 classic 'Breezin' blew a hole in mainstream listening charts.

**Perhaps the biggest name in jazz guitar today.**

# 6. Al Di Meola (b.1954)

Speed demon. Plays Gibsons - ES175 and Les Paul – plus he's an Ovation endorsee. Discovered in the early '70s by **Chick Corea**, and invited to join jazz supergroup 'Return to Forever'. Toured and recorded with **John McLaughlin** and **Paco de Lucia**. Developed a distinctive speed style combining virtuoso musicianship with a need to shine technically.

Not always appreciated by his contemporaries, Di Meola maintains a purity in his solo playing – e.g. 1985 acoustic 'Cielo E Terra'.

# 7. Pat Metheny (b.1954)

Jazz/Rock fusion legend and major ambassador for jazz guitar today. Uses Gibson ES175 and an Ibanez custom model. Has experimented with Roland GR300 guitar synth and also fretless guitars.

Became a music teacher whilst developing a live gig and recording career playing alongside **Ornette Coleman** and **Eberhard Weber**. Built bridges with folk and rock fans by accompanying **Joni Mitchell** and **David Bowie** (ask any non-jazz fan to name *one* jazz guitarist) and continues to experiment.

# 8. Stanley Jordan (b.1959)

Devised unusual two-handed tapping technique. Used various guitars, including Casio PG380 synth. Plays as if he's using a keyboard - right hand plays single notes, left hand covers chord.

Signed with Blue Note records in mid-80s and cut 'Stairway to the Rainbow' featuring his re-working of the **Led Zeppelin** classic.

Still working on new techniques, and still travelling down his own road.

# 9. John Scofield (b.1951)

Technical but tasteful. Uses Gibson ES335 and Ibanez Artist AS200. Famed for sparsity of style, allowing melody to breathe above his distinctive, customised sound - he likes to sneak up round the back of a traditional harmonic structure.

Played with **Charlie Mingus** and **Gerry Mulligan**. Later joined **Miles Davis** on tour and co-wrote with him.

Probably best known for 'Grace Under Pressure' on Blue Note (1992).

# 10. Martin Taylor (b.1956)

The only Brit in this list. Uses a Yahama custom model and a single cutaway Benedetto. Prolific performer with a stunning fingerstyle technique that impressed **Stephane Grappelli** enough to collaborate with him.

Also employs more traditional percussive picking style which makes him equally at home in a folk setting.

Recording success with 'Artistry' (1992). Formed Spirit Of Django quintet in 1994.

"OK cats, it's vamping on the one with pedal twos, then into the head on the nod..." Bandleader **Louis Armstrong** sure knew his bluff-speak.

# Bluff-Speak
## Jazz Jargon Translated

"OK cats, it's vamping on the one with pedal twos, then into the head on the nod. After the first pickup, trade licks when we hit fours, then blow until the stop solos. Take it a little outside if it's really cooking, but keep the changes the same until we're back to A. Jam straight eights after the first five turnarounds, then back round the head and out, staying inside all the way."

If the above phrases don't make any sense to you, it's because you aren't fluent in Jazz-speak. On these pages we've supplied a handy guide to all the commonly used jazz expressions.

| Jazz-Speak | Translation |
| --- | --- |
| **Cat** | Person |
| **Dude** | See 'Cat' |
| **Man** | Generally used as an alternative to commas in jazz-speak to give the speaker time to think (e.g. "check out the horn player man... that cat sure can blow") |
| **Lick** | Short musical phrase |
| **Trade licks** | Play phrases backwards and forwards between two musicians. Frequently taken to mean "play a phrase for as long as possible until someone else interrupts". |
| **Riff** | Repeating musical phrase, often forming the main part of a song |
| **Bread** | Fee (for an individual). As in "Any Bread?" (how much will I get paid?) |
| **The Bread** | Fee (for a band). As in "We ain't leavin' until we got The Bread" |
| **Jam** | Improvise |
| **Blow** | Improvise a solo |
| **Session** | A gathering of cats where licks occur, sometimes with bread, sometimes without |
| **Cooking** | Improvising exceptionally well. A cat will frequently jam and start cooking, even without any bread |
| **Sweet** | "I approve of your playing" (can also mean "yes, I will turn up on time to the next rehearsal") |

| | |
|---|---|
| **Inside** | Playing notes that fit with the current chord |
| **Outside** | Where you get thrown if you don't play notes that fit with the current chord |
| **Hot** | Fast |
| **Cool** | Slow |
| **Warm** | No treble on the amp |
| **Chilled** | Relaxed |
| **Stop solo** | Whole band plays a chord, then stops for couple of bars while someone takes a solo line |
| **Stop soloing** | What you have to do when the singer comes back in |
| **Changes** | Chords |
| **Chart** | Chord sheet |
| **Twos** | Notes worth two beats |
| **Fours** | Notes worth one beat |
| **Push** | Where the whole band plays ahead of the beat or barline |
| **The A** | The first section of the tune |
| **The B** | The second section of the tune |
| **On the nod** | At a given signal – usually used to change between the A and B section, or to signify the end of a section. |
| **Pedal** | Keeping the same bass note going over chords |
| **Horn** | Trumpet. Sometimes saxophone |
| **Standard** | A jazz tune that is so well known that all players are expected to be able to play it |
| **Real Book** | The Jazz Bible. Has charts and melody for most of the standards |
| **Singer** | Person that prevents you playing a guitar solo |
| **Head** | The main part of the tune, usually played before improvised solos |
| **Modal** | Improvising based in one key but using less obvious scales |
| **Vertical changes** | Chords which are not closely related to a constant home key |
| **Horizontal changes** | Long sections of chords that develop (as in standards) |
| **Straight** | Straight quavers |
| **Swung** | With a shuffle beat - every first note is slightly longer than every following note |
| **Pickup** | When the tune starts before the barline. Frequently played by solo instrument or sung |
| **Chromatic** | Note which lies between two inside tones |
| **Comping** | Playing chord backing on guitar. Short for 'accompanying'. |
| **Vamp until ready** | Keep comping until the singer or soloist comes in. |
| **Substitution** | Playing one chord instead of another to make a third chord (e.g. play Em7 instead of C and you imply C major 9th) |
| **Rhythm Cat** | Guitar player who doesn't know any scales |
| **Lead Cat** | Guitar player who never stops soloing |

# It's Easy To Bluff...
## Music and TAB Guide

Most guitar players can't read music. There. We've said it. So you can stop feeling guilty about it and get on with the serious business of pretending that you can. On these two pages you'll find tab and treble clef notation for all of the techniques featured in this book, along with tips on how to play them.

---

**HOW TO READ TREBLE CLEF:** The note on the bottom line of the treble clef is middle E – that is, it's the E which is found on the 2nd fret of the D string. The top line is F (1st fret, high E string).

Guitar notes that are lower or higher than this range are notated using 'leger lines' – these are extra stave lines drawn in above or below the main clef.

---

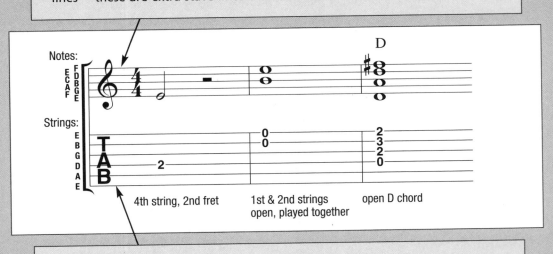

Notes:

Strings:

4th string, 2nd fret     1st & 2nd strings open, played together     open D chord

---

**HOW TO READ TAB:** The six lines represent the strings – the thickest (lowest) string is at the bottom. The number shows the fret.

---

**HOW TO READ CHORD PARTS:** The chord names are written above, and sometimes the musical rhythm of the part is notated underneath.

If no rhythm is given, or you see several even 'slashes' in a bar, then normally you should make up your own rhythm pattern. If you see two chords in a bar, it's normally assumed that they're played for two beats each.

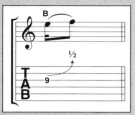

**SEMITONE BEND (OR HALF-STEP BEND):** Play the note with the picking hand then bend it up a semitone (so it reaches the pitch of the note on the next fret).

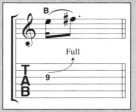

**WHOLE TONE BEND:** Duh! Just bend it further!

**GRACE NOTE BEND:** The only difference with these is that you start bending as soon as you've picked the note. You should hardly hear the first note.

**QUARTER-TONE BEND:** Just bend the string a little – don't go as far as a semitone. Quarter-tone is used to mean any bend that's less than a semitone.

**BEND AND RELEASE:** Play the note, bend it up, let it back down again.

**PRE-BEND:** Bend the note up before you play it.

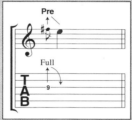

**PRE-BEND AND RELEASE:** Bend the note up, then play it, then release the bend while the note rings on.

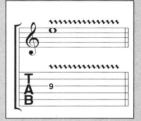

**VIBRATO:** Move the string up and down by rapidly bending and releasing it by a small amount.

**HAMMER-ON:** Pick one note, then sound the higher note by fretting it without re-picking. Hammer-ons are always ascending in pitch.

**PULL-OFF:** Get both fingers into the positions shown in the tab, then pick the higher note. Whilst it rings on, pull the finger off the string to sound the lower note.

**SLIDE/GLISS:** While the note is sounding, slide the fretting finger up or down to the position shown in the tab.

**SLIDE/GLISS AND RESTRIKE:** As before, but this time repick the second note after you've finishing sliding.

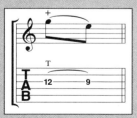

**TAPPING:** Fret the note using the picking hand by tapping onto the position shown. Usually followed by a pull-off.

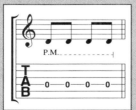

**PALM MUTING:** Rest the picking hand on the strings very near to the bridge. This partially mutes the notes – the technique is used a lot in blues and rock rhythm playing.

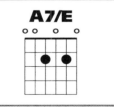

**A7/E**

**SLASH CHORDS:** Many players get confused when they see chord notation like this for the first time. Do not fear – it's simple. The letter name before the slash is the chord you play. The one after the slash is the bass note. Bluffing tip - if you find it too difficult to play a particular bass note at the same time as the chord, try ignoring it and just playing the chord, then get a bassist or keyboard player to supply the bottom end.

The great **Tal Farlow** – fond of a 9th chord or several

# Cool Chords or 'How does he do that with only four fingers?'

Most jazz guitarists spend 90% of their time playing accompaniment, or 'comping'. So why do they concentrate on solos and ignore their rhythm playing? In this section, you'll discover some unusual chords (or new versions of simple chords) that rarely appear in chord books.

In each case we've supplied tips on when to use the chord, plus some ideas on how it could be incorporated into a rhythm part.

 # It's Easy To Bluff... 7th Chords

It's much easier to understand a chord like C#m(maj7) if you know how 7ths are constructed. The table below shows the four kinds of 7th chords used in jazz, together with the theory of how they're constructed, plus all the ways you'll commonly see them written in a chart. All the examples are shown with a root of C. Here's the science bit!

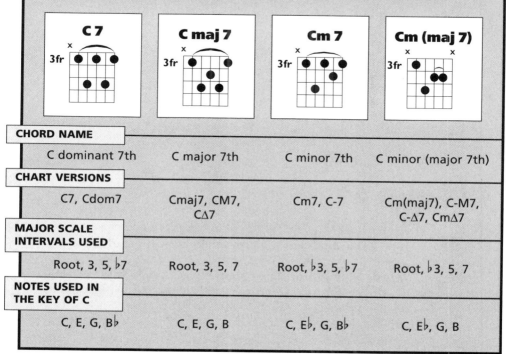

| | C 7 | C maj 7 | Cm 7 | Cm (maj 7) |
|---|---|---|---|---|
| **CHORD NAME** | C dominant 7th | C major 7th | C minor 7th | C minor (major 7th) |
| **CHART VERSIONS** | C7, Cdom7 | Cmaj7, CM7, C△7 | Cm7, C-7 | Cm(maj7), C-M7, C-△7, Cm△7 |
| **MAJOR SCALE INTERVALS USED** | Root, 3, 5, ♭7 | Root, 3, 5, 7 | Root, ♭3, 5, ♭7 | Root, ♭3, 5, 7 |
| **NOTES USED IN THE KEY OF C** | C, E, G, B♭ | C, E, G, B | C, E♭, G, B♭ | C, E♭, G, B |

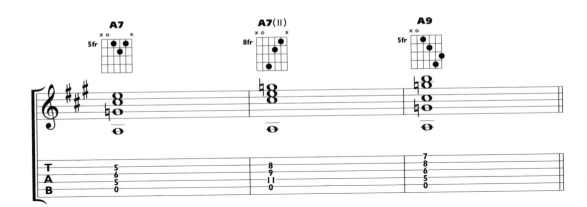

# 'Middle A7'

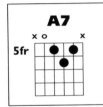

The 7th chord (properly called 'dominant 7th') is fundamental to all types of Blues and Jazz. This change from the basic open position voicing of A7 - as with all the chords on this page – can be moved to any key if you omit the open fifth string which provides the root in this case.

# 'Joe Pass A7'

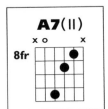

A different 'stacking' of the A7 chord. If you're going to bluff successfully, you need to know this kind of thing! Players like **Joe Pass** freely mix different voicings, often creating a melody line with the highest note of each shape.

# 'Tal Farlow A9'

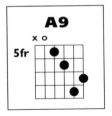

Where A7 fits, so will A9. An A7 chord has been altered to feature a B (the ninth note of the A major scale) as the top/melody note.

You will hear this kind of approach in **Tal Farlow**'s playing. Occasionally, he would even add extra notes with his picking hand fingers.

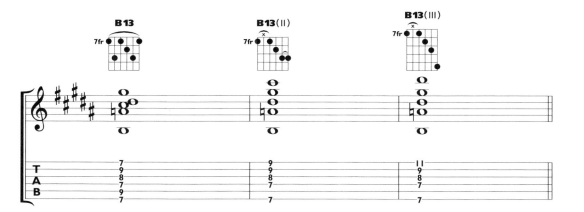

# 'Latin B13'

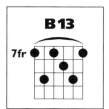

Once you've decided that you're going to extend a few chords, make sure you know enough to keep all rival bluffers asking "what was that chord?". This is B13 - basically a B7 chord with a G♯ (the 13th) on top. 13th chords evoke the Latin American sound of **Laurindo Almeida** and **Charlie Byrd**.

# 'Sliding B13'

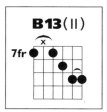

This version of B13 has the 9th (C♯) on top. This voicing is particularly effective when moving from the fret below or above, in a semitone shift - a trick all bluffers should know.

As with all the chords on this page, the fifth string is not used.

# 'Finger-breaking B13'

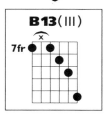

A very extended version of **Allan Holdsworth** proportions, this covers more than two octaves. Here, the 3rd (D♯) is the top/melody note. If you play all the chords on this page in order, it begins to sound rather clever.

**Tip – use this chord if you're ever photographed with a guitar.**

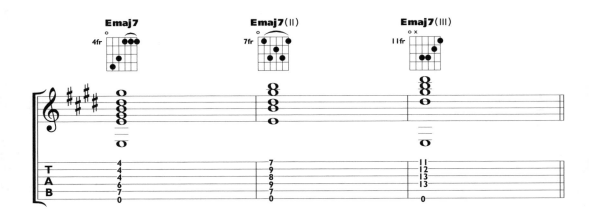

# 'Basic Emaj7'

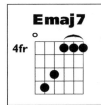

No self respecting jazzer would be without the Major 7th chord – they're also an essential part of countless Standards ('Autumn Leaves', 'Fly Me To The Moon' etc). This shape is moveable anywhere on the fingerboard, so long as you omit the sixth string.

Let the bass player earn his own keep!

# 'Easy Emaj7'

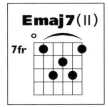

An alternative take on Emaj7 brings the melody/top note up to B, which suggests a more melodic approach, especially when mixed with other voicings. It is fairly easy to jump out of this chord for some high register noodlings, then back in just in time for the next change. This trick is guaranteed to impress even diehard pro players.

# 'Barney Kessel Emaj7'

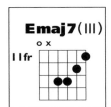

When you're feeling really confident, try interjecting this chord shape into single lines, perhaps even 'sweeping' across the strings with your pick/fingers, to add some **Barney Kessel**-type finesse to your solo lines.

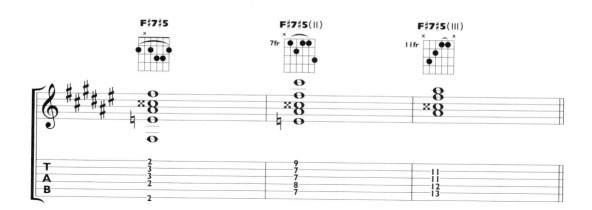

# 'Easy F♯7♯5'

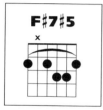

Wherever there are 7th chords, there are possibilities for endless substitutions or chord extensions. To hear this in context, play it 'resolving' to a B minor (7th of course). There are some lovely possibilities for expert-sounding solo lines over this sequence too. ♯5 chords are sometimes called 'augmented' chords.

# 'Russell Malone F♯7♯5'

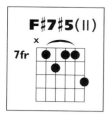

With the 7th note (E) on the bottom, there is a different feel to this inversion of the chord. Even when the bass player is hitting the root, you can change the 'focus' of the overall sound. **Russell Malone** is fond of this approach.

# 'High register F♯7♯5'

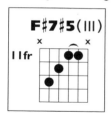

Played high up the neck, a shape like this is easily moveable, giving the possibility of quick changes, or weaving in and out of solo lines. This approach is a **Barney Kessel** fave.

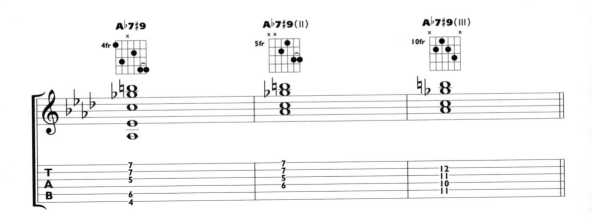

# 'Classic A♭7♯9'

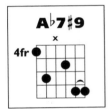

This *really* cool chord is a favourite with all jazz players, and you'll hear it in many classic tunes.

There is some nice dissonant work featuring this chord at the beginning of **Tal Farlow**'s 'Falling In Love With Love'.

# 'Narrow A♭7♯9'

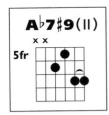

Here's a 'narrower' but more easily moveable version of the same chord. It lends itself more to comping and rhythmic punches.

You can never know enough voicings of this kind of chord.

# 'Low A♭7♯9'

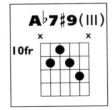

This is the most 'dark' sounding voicing of this chord, perhaps best for a picked single note approach, so it avoids becoming muddy instead of mysterious!

Once again, it is moveable to any key.

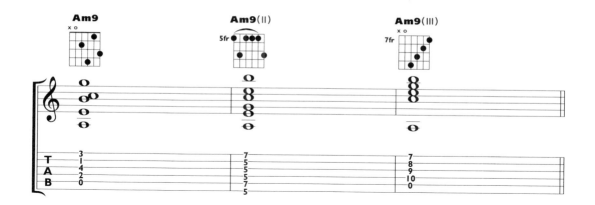

# 'Experimental Am9'

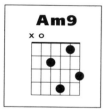

An exotic sounding chord, that calls to mind some of the experimental work of **Al Di Meola** and **Eric Johnson**.

With the open fifth string omitted, this shape can be transposed to any key easily - once your fingers have got used to it.

# 'Wide Am9'

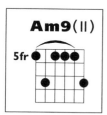

A big, open sounding voicing which uses all six strings in any key.

Experiment with lifting the B (or 9th) off periodically to produce melodic results. Just pretend there is a complicated harmonic reason for doing it...

# 'Larry's Am9'

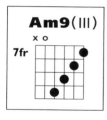

In the key of A, the open fifth string provides a convenient root, but this would probably become redundant in a band/comping situation.

Using the top four strings, this voicing is great for superimposing over a 'straight' A minor chord – a favourite trick of **Larry Carlton**.

# How Not To Be Frightened
# By A Chord Chart - the 5 and 9 trick

If a rock/blues player sees the chord name '7th' on a chart, they rarely get worried. After a little while chords like 9ths, minor 9ths and even 13ths become second nature. But what do you do if you see a half-bar change to C#7(♭5#9)? Surely no-one's brain works that fast?

Well, no. But think about it – what actually *is* a C#7(♭5#9)? It's basically a C#7 (not too tough, I hope?) with the 5th played one fret lower (flattened), and a 9th played one fret higher (sharpened). So wouldn't it be cool if there was an easy 7th shape where you could just move the 5ths and 9ths around as you wanted, to save learning loads of complex chords?

**There is. Here it is, shown in all its possibilities, based around a 5th fret chord of D7.**

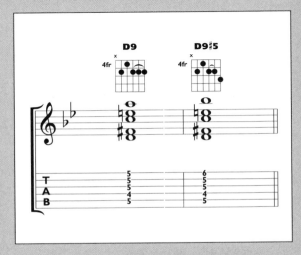

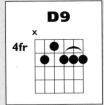

A real staple chord of the genre, the 9th chord is one of those awkward shapes that require your 3rd or 4th finger to be flattened, or to barre the top three strings. This seems impossible at first, but soon becomes second nature. Now remember – the 9th is played on the 2nd (B) string; the 5th is played on the first (top E) string. You will need to know this to play the following chord...

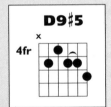

So here's our first change. We're taking the 5th note (played on the 1st string, remember) and moving it up a fret, creating a #5.

This kind of chord is dissonant on its own, and usually needs to resolve to another chord. Try G minor or D7.

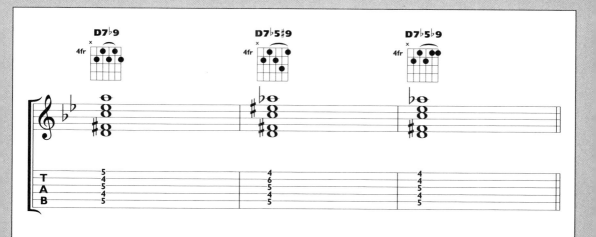

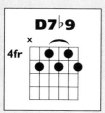

Here, we need to refinger the chord slightly, but the idea's the same. The 9th note (played on the 2nd string) is simply dropped back a fret. This is a wonderful chord for resolving to Gm9, so never approach a copy of 'The Real Book' without it. Imagine playing spine tingling improvisations over this while the band hold the chord at the end of a number. By the time you resolve to Gm9, you will be every jazzer's hero.

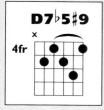

Drop the 5th, raise the 9th, and you've got this HardBopper's favourite.

This kind of dramatic chord has been used often on film scores. It's hard to believe there is a basic D7 chord hidden under there.

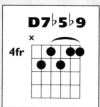

Because of the first finger barre, this chord's easier than it looks.

Combine it with D7(♭9) and Gm7, and you have the recipe for a classic jazz progression. Using just three fingers, you can have other aspiring jazz guitarists squinting to try and work out what you are doing!

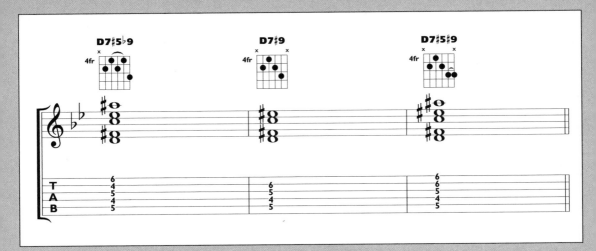

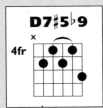

**D7♯5♭9**

Raise the 5th, lower the 9th, and you get this beauty.

Combine it with D7(♭9) and D7(♭5♭9) and you will begin to hear how some players create such wide soundscapes with apparently little effort. The top note can be a very effective melody line for chordal soloing or comping.

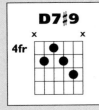

**D7♯9**

Perhaps the most widely known of these altered chords (due to a certain **James Marshall Hendrix**), this combination of major and minor tonalities never seems to date and is as experimental sounding now as it was in the 40s and 50s.

Don't forget to mute the 1st string.

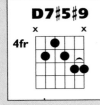

**D7♯5♯9**

Raise both intervals by flattening the little finger.

This one's just begging to have some 'outside' Bop lines played over it. Again, it's a nice easy shape considering the scary name.

# Chord Charts
## or 'How am I supposed to play six chords in one bar?'

**Whatever kind of jazz you want to play, it's a dead cert that you're going to have to read a chart at some time. In this section there are 6 fairly simple chord sequences, laid out as you'd see them at a jazz gig.**

For each chord sequence we've put the basic, simple chords in the stave, and a 'bluffed' version above in fretboxes, which contains jazzy alternatives to the basic chords. Use these ideas to demonstrate your mastery of harmonic theory next time you're given a chord sheet...

 ## Chord Tips

- Remember that jazz players *very* rarely play full 6-string chords throughout a track. More often, they use partial chords. When you try a new chord, take great care to mute the unwanted strings.
- **Using a plectrum gives a lot of control over the rhythm, but makes it harder to control muted strings.**
- On the other hand (well, on the same hand actually), fingerstyle is generally more difficult, and limits the volume you can get out of an acoustic.
- **Try to avoid harsh, bright guitar tones. Comping generally uses a soft-ish sound, so try neck or middle pickup positions to start with.**
- If you're getting fret buzz, move the fingers along so they're just behind the fret. This means you can get away with less pressure from the fretting hand.
- **If you're going to work with a bass player, remember, you don't *have* to play the bass note of the chord.**
- Don't use distortion for chord parts. Just don't. Ever!
- **Use the heaviest strings you can stand. Really light strings are more likely to be bent out of tune when you're trying out an unfamiliar chord.**
- If you see two chords in a bar, these are 'half-bar' changes (so in 4/4 time, you'd play them for two beats each). These take some getting used to, but are essential if you're going to be a good 'comper'.
- **Four chords in a bar means one change every beat. When you see this in a chart, practise the bar over and over before you try the whole piece.**

# 'Substituted 7ths'

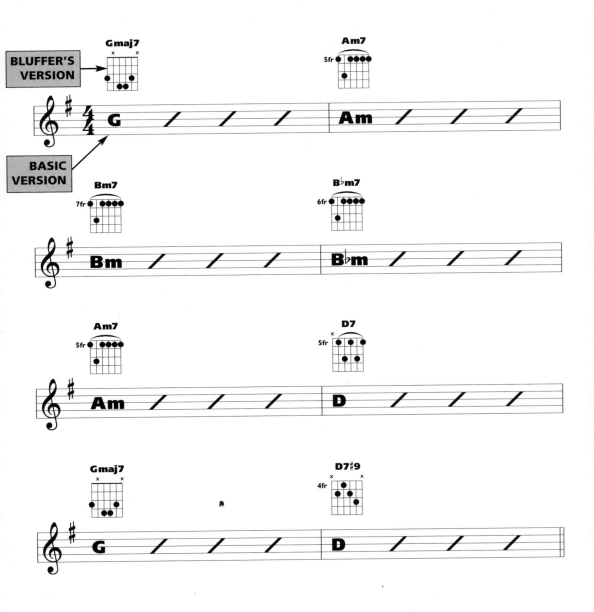

The first step along the road to jazz heaven is to add the dominant 7th to straight major or minor chords. This is generally the accepted practice in all jazz. This chart goes one step further, making the G into a major 7th chord for even jazzier results. In the last bar, the D7#9 makes a nice parting shot.

# 'More Movement'

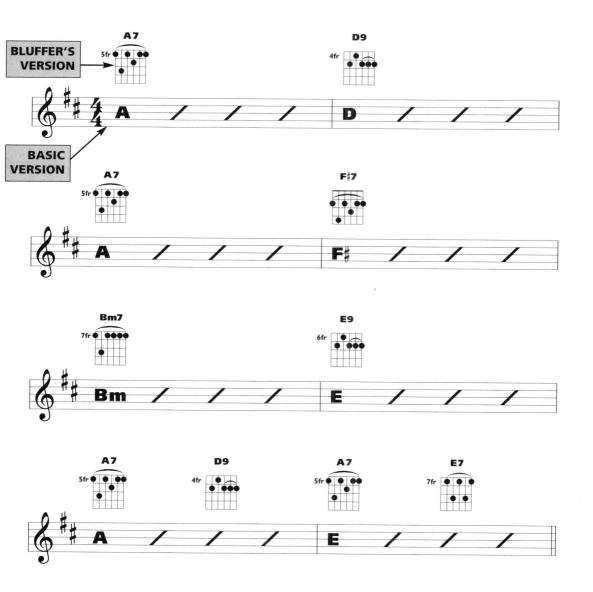

After the inevitable A7 beginning, the D is replaced by a D9. The F$\sharp$ is here replaced by a seventh, but imagine the fear if you were to read a complex chord such as F$\sharp$7$\flat$9 here. The last two bars are split to give a bit more movement, using 7th and 9th chords.

# 'Meddling With Minors'

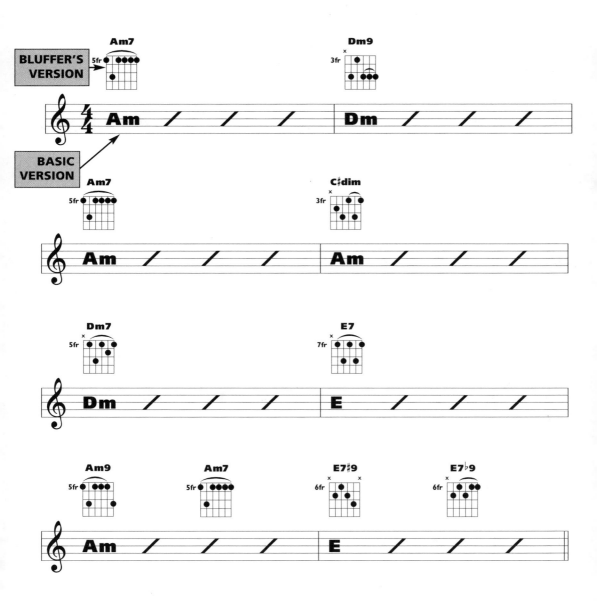

After an Am7 start, the Dm9 gives an interesting chord change, while retaining the same top note (A). The fourth bar uses a C♯ diminished chord as an alternative to another bar of Am, leading sweetly to the Dm7. The last two bars show a little melodic movement with the Am9 - Am7, and again with E7♯9 to E7♭9.

# 'Getting More Complex'

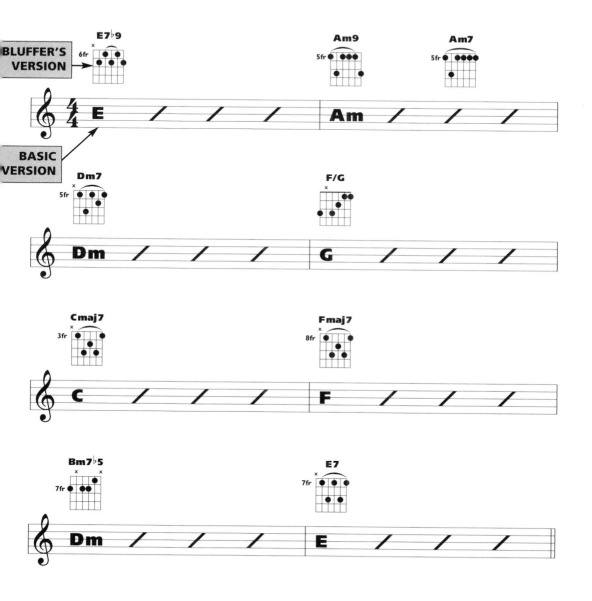

Using the E7(♭9) as a dramatic lead in, the Am9 – Am7 again provides a melody. The fourth bar features an F/G 'slash' chord. This means an F chord is played over a G bass note, giving a nice variation from G7 (it actually implies G dominant 11th, theory fans). The C and Fmaj7 chords are followed by a Bm7(♭5), which could be viewed in this case as a Dm/B slash chord. Yet another string to your bluffer's bow...

# 'Half-Bar Substitutions'

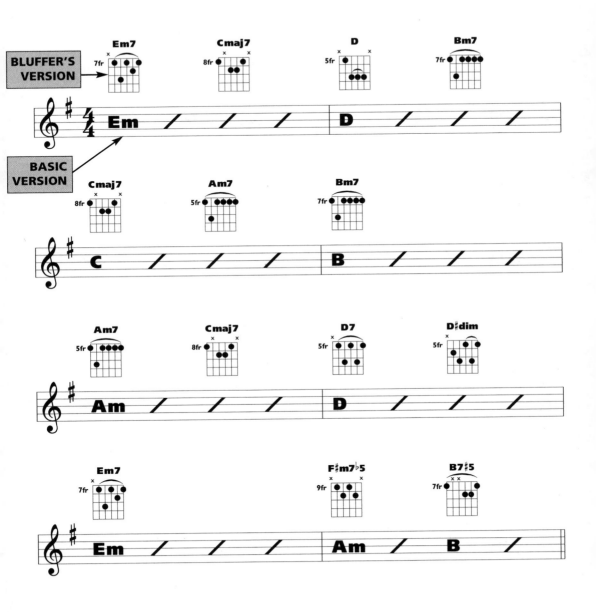

This one begins with a change from Em7 to Cmaj7 (think about it – add a note of C to Em and you get Cmaj7, so the chords are great substitutions for each other). D follows through to its relative minor, Bm7, then Cmaj7 to its relative minor Am7. After a bar of B7, this is reversed (Am7 to Cmaj7), then a D7 and D♯ diminished gives a chromatically ascending bassline to Em7. The last two bars are a turnaround, taking you back to the start of the sequence.

# 'Half-Bar Chromatics'

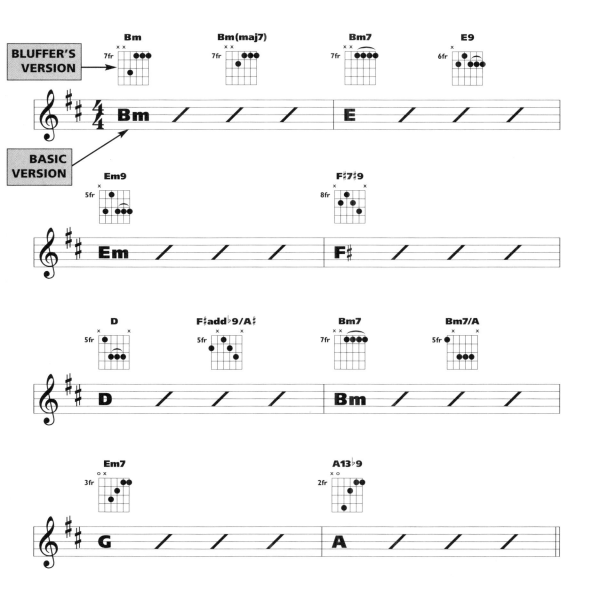

Playing through the first four chords now gives a chromatic descending line
on the fourth string. This continues into the Em9 in the third bar. The plain F♯ major
is exchanged for a more exciting F♯7(♯9), followed by some passing chords;
the F♯(add♭9)/A leads nicely into the Bm7 and Bm7/A. Next is an Em7 chord
(which expert bluffers will notice is simply a G chord with an E bass note). The last
A13(add♭9) adds a certain tension before the progression rolls round again...

**Barney Kessel** knew there was no substitute for a good chord substitution.

# Chord Substitution or 'Why are you playing all the wrong chords?'

**If you spend any time around jazzers you'll hear them talk about 'substitution'. Don't worry – it doesn't mean they're going to sack you and get a better guitar player. It refers to the practice of playing one chord instead of another to imply a third chord.**

So if, say, the chart suggests a chord of Am (which contains notes of A, C and E) and the guitar plays C (C, E and G), the implied chord (A,C, E and G) is Am7. Obviously it's tricky to do this at speed, so in this section we've supplied some common examples of how it's achieved.

The first four examples demonstrate substitutions of the I ('one'), IV ('four'), and V ('five') chord. In the key of A, these are A, D and E. For maximum jazziness, all chords have been played as sevenths or ninths in the examples.
The table below shows some of the possibilities for substituting in the key of A.

| Position in scale (A Major) | Chord Name | Substitute with... | To create... | When to use it |
|---|---|---|---|---|
| I | A, Amaj7 | C#m7 | Amaj9 | Vamping on the I chord, or returning to the I chord |
| I(7) | A7 | Em | A9 | Vamping on the I chord, or just before moving to the IV |
| I (minor) | Am, Am7 | Cmaj7 | Am9 | Any minor key chart |
| IV | D, Dmaj7 | F#m7 | Dmaj9 | Whenever you're playing the IV chord (not as effective in bluesy sequences) |
| IV (minor) | Dm | F | Dm7 | Any minor key chart |
| V7 | E7 | G#dim7 | E7($\flat$9) | Whenever V chord is a 7th |

# 'Substituting The I'

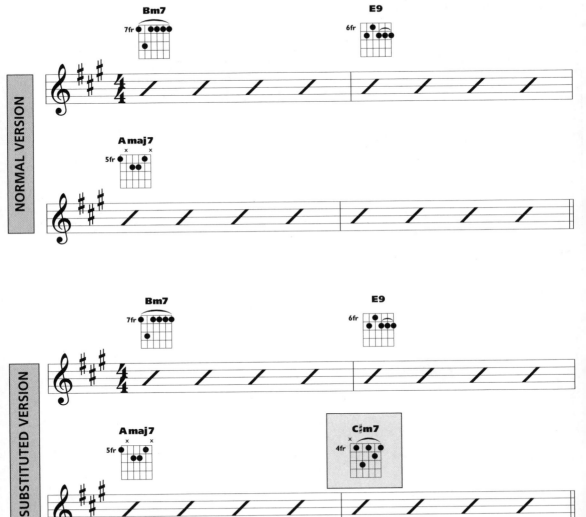

There are no rules when substituting - just make sure the melody line still fits and that it sounds tasteful. Here, the I chord (Amaj7) has been replaced by the III minor 7 (C#min7).

# 'Substituting The IV'

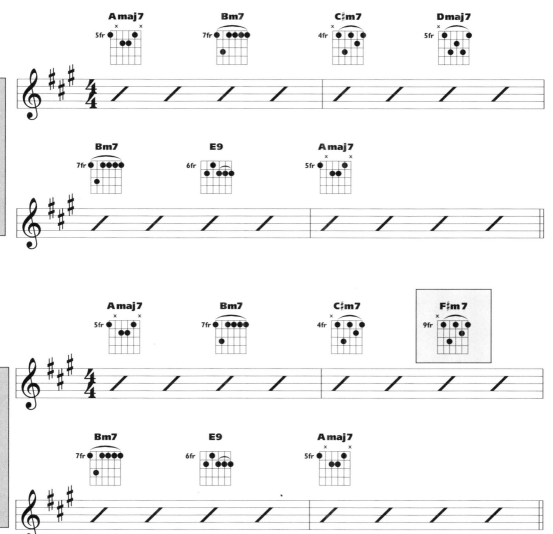

**NORMAL VERSION**

**SUBSTITUTED VERSION**

Staying in the key of A, here the IV chord (Dmaj7) has been changed to the VI minor 7 chord (F#m7). This takes away some of the predictability of the original progression by implying Dmaj9, especially when used as an *occasional* alternative.

# 'Substituting The V'

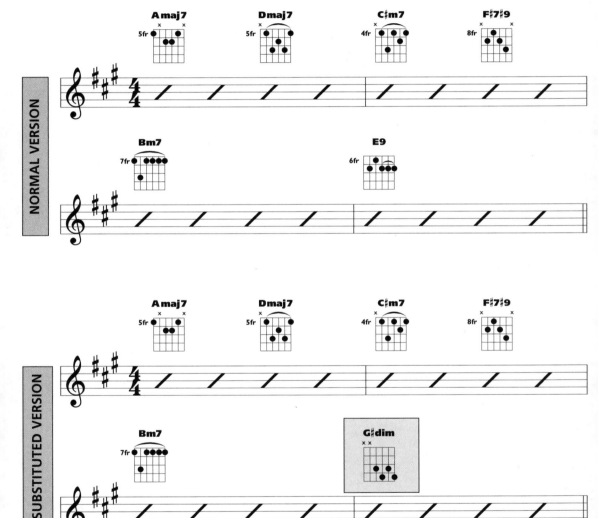

By changing the V chord (E9) for the VII diminished (G# diminished) this set of changes loses some of its nursery-rhyme feel and becomes a little more dramatic. Certainly better for showing off your knowledge of obscure scales. You're actually implying E7♭9 here.

# 'II-V-I'

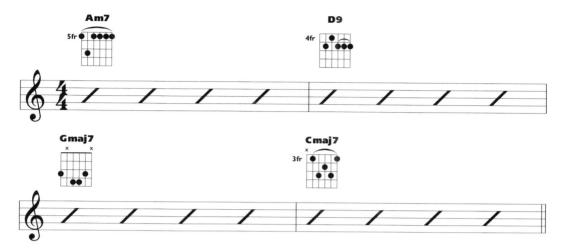

The two-five-one change (e.g. Dm-G-C) is the most important chord sequence in jazz. This example uses extended chords in G major - in this case Am7, D9 and Gmaj7. This idea occurs in the jazz standard 'All The Things You Are'.

# 'II-V-I with a key change'

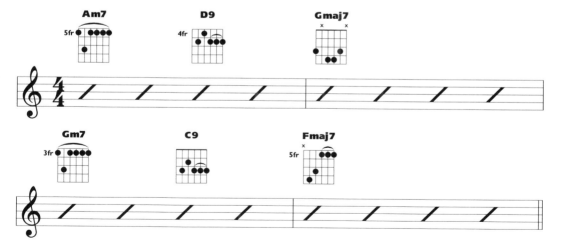

Here, the previous example is played double-time, then the exact same chords are played two frets lower. If you can play a solo over these changes, you're really starting to understand jazz harmony properly (**tip** – solo over the first two bars using the G major scale, then the last two using the F major scale).

# 'Repeating II-V'

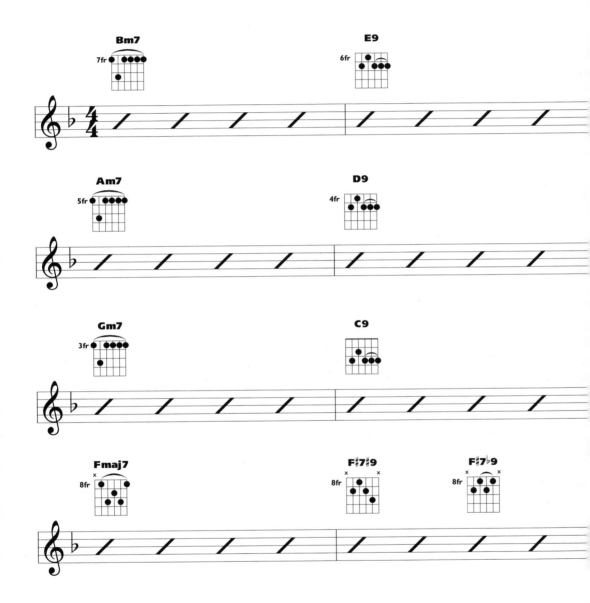

If you constantly play II-V changes without ever returning to the I chord, you're creating the kind of harmony that really makes jazz solos 'move'. This sequence is based around the home key of F major, and descends first through the key of A (so the II-V is Bm-E) and G (so the II-V is Am-D). The beauty of a progression like this is that once you know the shapes, you can amaze all those present by moving the same two-chord lick down two frets each time. **Joe Pass** does this masterfully on his version of 'Night And Day'.

# 'Repeating Chromatic II-V'

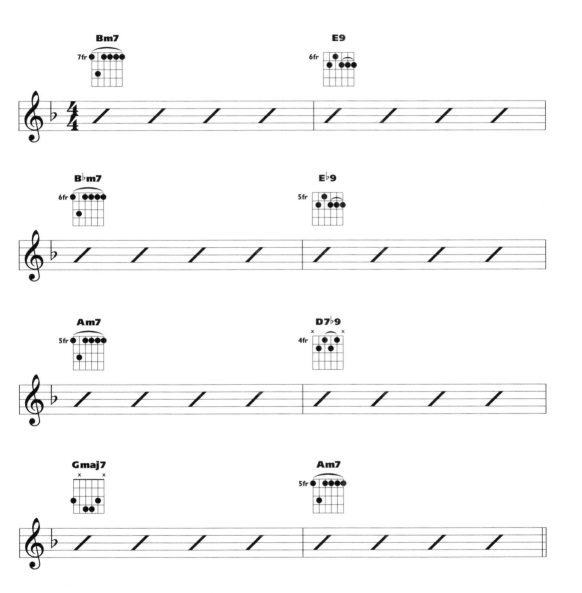

This is just the kind of II-V progression you would hear **Jimmy Raney** or **Charlie Parker** playing over. This time, the key cycles down in semitones, which can fool the listener into thinking it's far more complicated than it really is.

**Herb Ellis'** jazz licks were often tinted a shade of blue…

# Lead Licks or 'Why can't I just play one scale all the time?'

**Enough of this chord nonsense – I want to take a solo! Unfortunately, the jazz player has to work a lot harder than any rock guitarist in order to 'play lead'. Our leather-clad cousins simply stomp on a fuzz pedal, assume the essential legs-apart position, and play hammer-ons as fast as possible up and down a simple scale shape.**

In jazz, we have to think a little differently, because our playing always has to take account of the backing chords. Even if we hit a wild, wrong-sounding note deliberately, it only sounds that way because of its relationship to the harmony. There are a few vital things to remember when you're playing jazz lead.

# Bluff Your Way Through a Solo

- **Know the harmony. Always make sure you know what the current chord is, and play solo lines which are related to it.**
- Use phrasing. Take musical breaks every four bars or so to let the audience digest what they've just heard. Even Fusion players do this (well, occasionally).
- **Go for 'target' notes. Decide on which note you want each lick / phrase to finish on before you start to play it (and relate it to the chord backing). Even if you hit a bum note, you'll always end up somewhere musical.**
- Play round the arpeggios, not just the home scale. Use notes of the current chord wherever you can.
- **Use chromatics. If you're playing a lick which ends on a note of A, try playing a note of A♭ or A♯ just before it. It's dead simple to do, but it works almost every time.**
- Use rhythmic displacement. This means playing the same notes (say, a four-note lick) over and over, but occurring at different times in the bar. It can create very complex-sounding ideas with very little effort.
- **Use dynamics. Who says you have to play every note at the same volume?**
- Use parallel 4ths. The simplest way to do this is to play a tune on the B or E string, flattening the finger over both and sliding it up and down. If you get away with it, it can sound very Bebop.
- **Use call-and-response. If you hear another band member play a lick and your ear is quick enough to work it out, then play it back at them. This duel-style soloing is a great crowd-pleaser.**

# 'Blue Herb'

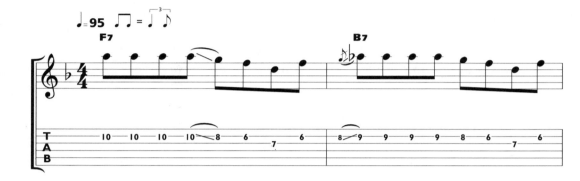

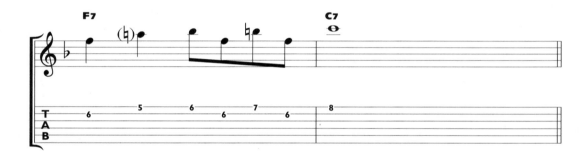

This **Herb Ellis**-style bluesy lick takes a chromatic approach, following the top notes of each chord. This approach is taken a little further in the third bar with a run up to the final note of C.

# 'Django's Changes'

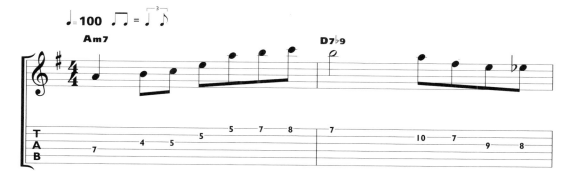

Based around the style of **Django Reinhardt**, this lick uses the A minor scale until halfway through the second bar, where the Gmaj7 chord is anticipated with a chromatic run, ending with a neat little Bm triad, which is really G major 7 without the bass note.

# 'Release The Tension'

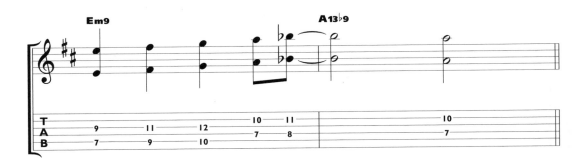

This cool **Wes Montgomery**-style lick is played in octaves, with an ascending feel. There is a 'tension and release' feel about the held notes in bars 2 and 4.

There is nothing wrong with dissonance, as long as you resolve it (or convince your audience it was deliberate).

# 'Swing In Time'

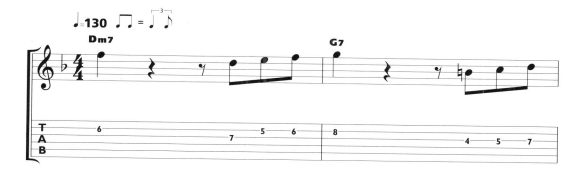

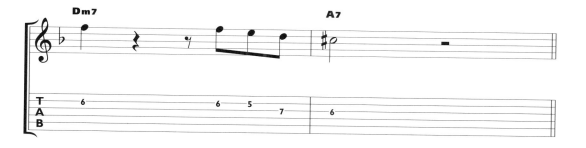

This Swing-style phrase is reminiscent of **Charlie Christian**. As well as choosing the right notes, don't forget to play them at the right time.

 **Take A Rest!**

Sometimes the best thing to play is nothing - this also gives you time to think out your next bluff!

# 'Suggest A Chord'

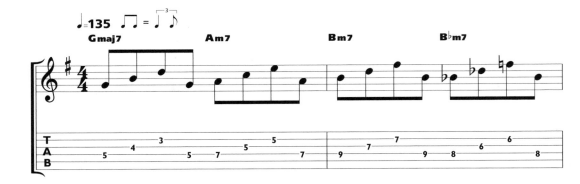

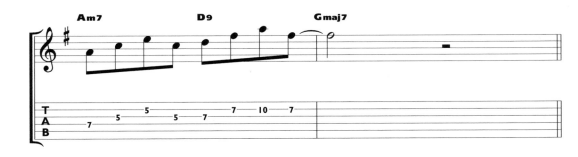

Following the changes with chord triads, this **George Benson** style phrase could hold its own without the chords behind it.

Note how the maj7th note (F♯) is targeted right over that final G chord. **Mmmm... nice!**

# 'Steal From The Best'

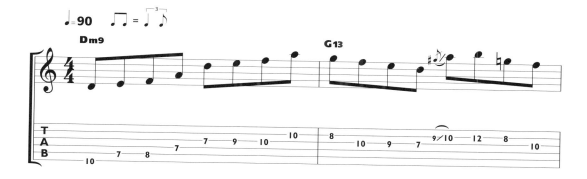

The constant motion of improvisers like **Charlie Parker** is the main influence here.

# Take Note

This example imitates itself between bars 2 and 3. This is the sign of
a consummate improviser, so remember to have a few stock licks like this in
reserve, when you want to get really 'spontaneous'...

# 'Help From Robben'

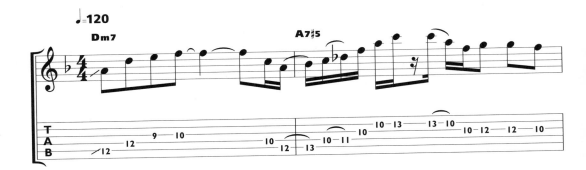

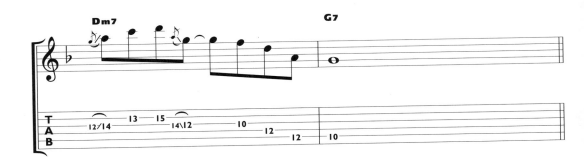

Similar to **Robben Ford**'s phrasing on 'Help The Poor', this phrase makes the most of the A7(♯5) chord. In a situation like this, the notes leading to and from the most difficult part of the phrase are secondary.

So you can afford to play it safe, as long as you can nail the difficult part.

# 'Arpeggio From Laura'

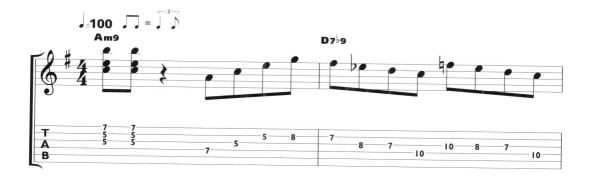

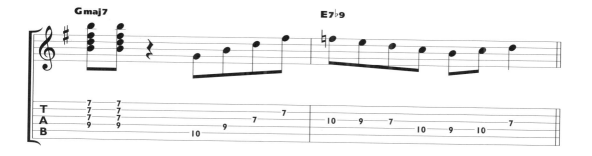

This one's similar to some of **Barney Kessel**'s phrasing in 'Laura'. It uses heavily accented chord stabs, punctuated with lines built around the chord tones.

If you choose notes from the chord when improvising you won't go far wrong.

# 'Cat's Chordal Cradle'

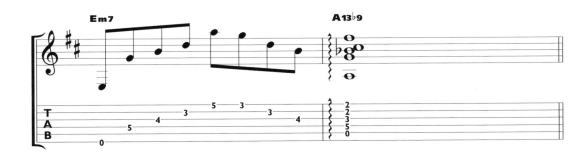

This intertwining of chords and melody is equally at home on unaccompanied guitar as it is with a full band backing. **Joe Pass** used this approach on tracks like 'Cherokee'. Here, it's not the speed that is important, it's the continuity.

Practise this one slowly until it's really smooth.

# 'Sack The Bass Player'

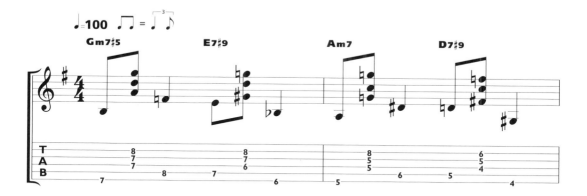

Players like **Martin Taylor** have amazed audiences by arranging chord progressions with their own walking basslines.

This might not be as mind boggling as his famous version of 'I Got Rhythm', but it gives you a good idea of some of the tricks of this technique i.e. arranging short chord stabs to imply the chords rather than trying to be in too many places at once.

**Scott Henderson**'s chromatic approach to playing over changes
can be tricky to keep up with...

# Playing Over Changes or 'How do I read the chart and play lead at the same time?'

The principle is so simple. All you need to do is play notes which fit with the chord being played. Only two things make life difficult. Firstly, you need to construct a meaningful melody while you do it, and secondly, you need to work out the arpeggios and licks at speed while the changes are flying past.

Now you've developed some of the techniques shown in the previous chapter (i.e. thinking about arpeggio notes and selecting 'target' notes for licks), let's start really thinking about those chords.

Too many guitarists still start a solo from the point of view of a scale. You know the kind of thing; **"I can use D Dorian here, but then it has to be Lydian flat 7 over the #11 chord..."**. A jazzer thinks much more in terms of the chord content, and then tries to anticipate how his or her note choices will sound over these changes.

# How to do it

Try this – record yourself playing some of the changes in this chapter, or get a friend to play them as accompaniment. Now try making up a solo using only notes from the arpeggio of the current chord.

As the chord changes, change to another arpeggio and so on. It'll probably sound a bit forced and mechanical at first, but remember you can use any rhythmic values, and you can vary the duration of any note at any time, as long as you stay within the arpeggio notes.

Once you've mastered this with a simple sequence, try adding 'passing notes' – i.e. notes that aren't part of the current arpeggio – in between the arpeggio tones. This way, you're always going to (or coming from) a note which 'works'. Keep going round and round a sequence using these two ideas, and you'll soon find yourself creating melodic lines that *really* sound like jazz.

# 'Bop Round The Head'

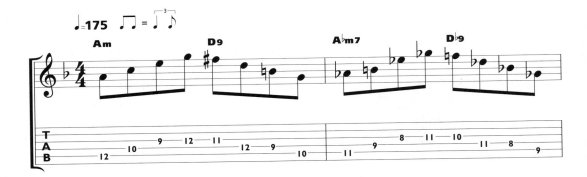

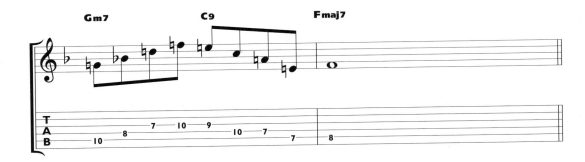

This typical Bop lick over changes is reminiscent of **Tal Farlow**, amongst others. The chromatic chord movement is mirrored by the arpeggiated solo line.

There is a passing note at the end of bars 1 and 2, anticipating the next chord.

# 'Show No Fear'

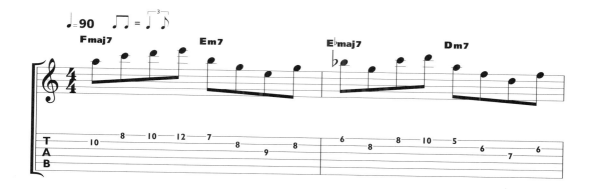

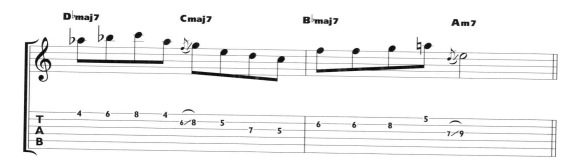

At first glance, this descending chord phrase is an improviser's worst nightmare!

However, carefully following the chords and varying the phrasing to avoid too obvious a pattern developing creates a sophisticated sounding phrase.

 # Take Note

Check out the linear movement across the strings, as opposed to 'position' playing.

# 'Nail It Fast'

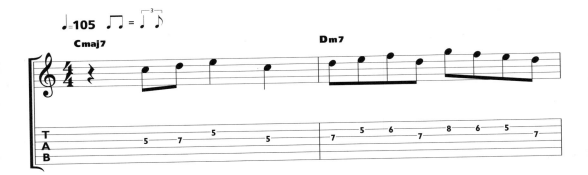

Here, again, the key is to nail as many chord tones as you can. This phrase takes a **John Scofield** type approach to the ascending chords.

The more confident you become, the quicker you can play weird licks, and the further 'outside' you can go.

# 'Simple – Or Is It?'

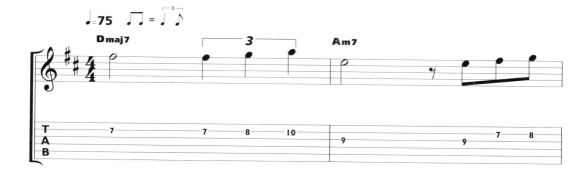

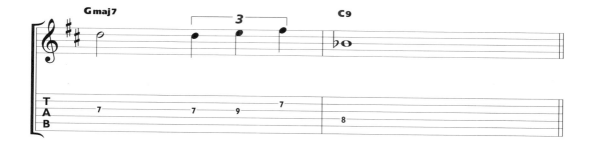

This one's easy on the face of it, but you need to know your chords to be able to *improvise* a phrase like this. It uses scale fragments for each chord, then follows up with a chord tone at the beginning of each bar.

Before you know it, a melody begins to develop. This is known as advanced, or black belt, bluffing.

# 'Scott & Allan Have A Cup Of Tea'

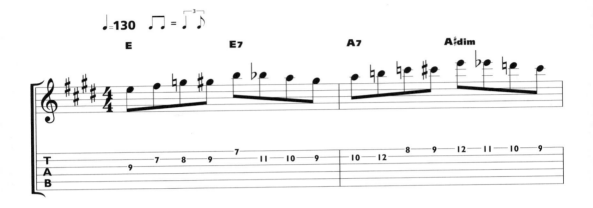

Using constant quavers in a swung rhythm, this example weaves its way round the chords in a style similar to (but considerably slower than) **Scott Henderson**. If you use more hammer-ons and pull-offs, it starts to take on an **Allan Holdsworth** feel.

Either way, it's surprising how often you can get away with licks like this.

# 'Bum Of The Flighty Bee'

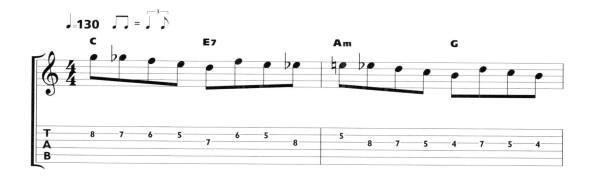

Now, we're getting so chromatic that (as far as the listener's concerned) we're almost leaving the changes behind. This lick is very adaptable, so feel free to make alterations until it suits your style and sound.

Choosing a logical fingering is the most difficult part.

# 'French Connections'

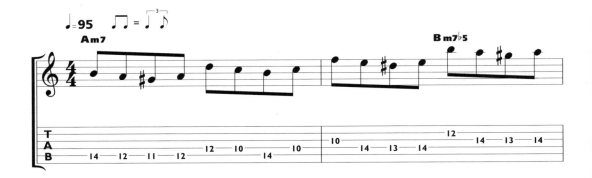

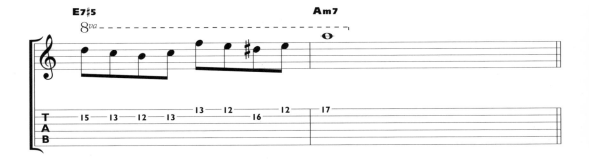

An almost classical sounding ascending line, this lick has definite **Django** overtones.

Although there is a distinct pattern here, as long as the final note is in key, the journey there can take many different routes.

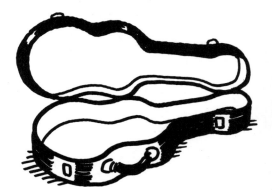

# 'Licks Without Frontiers'

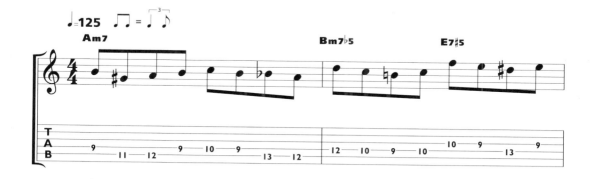

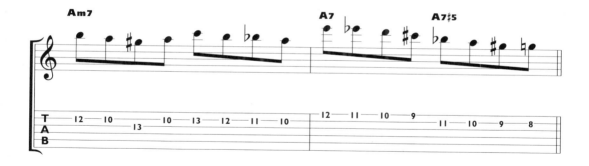

Take away the backing chords and you will find very little to link up the component parts of this phrase. This lick sounds bizarre enough for the likes of **John McLaughlin**, but traditional enough to crop up during a **Charlie Christian** improvisation.

It's designed to raise eyebrows at gigs, so use it!

Despite his pop success and contemporary sound, **Lee Ritenour** is as jazzy as they come.

# Selected Scales

To finish off, here are four essential scales you should know in order to cement your status as a jazz expert.

## 'The Jazz Minor'

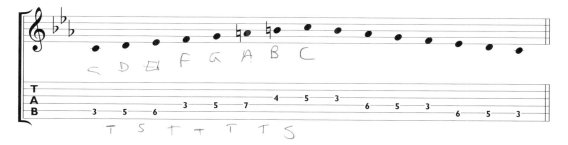

Known in classical circles as the 'Ascending Melodic Minor', this scale works a treat over any minor or minor 7th chord.

## 'The Whole Tone Scale'

Taking its name from the fact that all the notes are a tone apart, this scale is perfect for use over 7(#5) chords. However, you may find it impossible to fit anywhere else.

# 'The Diminished Scale'

Not only does this scale work beautifully over the diminished chord, it also sounds great over many V chord substitutions. Formed entirely from alternating whole tone/half tone steps, it forms an easily remembered pattern across the fingerboard.

# 'The Chromatic Scale'

Because it uses ALL the notes, this scale can begin or end anywhere you like, as long as you feel it works. Usually, ending on the root or a chord tone is sufficient to satisfy the most ardent jazz critic that you know exactly what you are doing. It's open to abuse pretty much anywhere.

# Music Shop Classic or 'How can I fit everything in this book into 48 bars of showing off?'

This custom-designed showpiece should amaze any onlookers and cynical staff at your local guitar shop. It's been specially devised to show off your technique whilst demonstrating your understanding of the styles of the greats. Watch the guy at the till nod knowingly as the player you're 'paying tribute to' (ahem) changes every 8 bars...

## Bar-by-bar breakdown

Opening with a turn-of-the-century style blues, move through the '30s with a nod to **Django** and **Eddie Lang** on the way. For the '40s and '50s take a dose of Django, laced with a shot of **Charlie Christian** and some of those well-loved horn-style arrangements. Then stroll into the late '50s section with those hip, experimental, Bebop-style chords. Sit up straight as you hit the '70s and bring in all that Fusion feel. Keep up the typical jazz chord structures, but introduce some dissonant combinations – this'll stop you getting too comfortable before the big free time finish, where you can really show off. Easy when you know how.

 ## Stay Cool!

First of all, be sure to play it at a tempo which enables you to make all the position shifts evenly. It's far better to nail a lick perfectly at a slower tempo than make a mess of it at high speed (unless you're playing *very* fast, that is, in which case any old rubbish will do).

At no point should you show undue strain, so make sure you're so well-practised that you can play it without breaking into a sweat. That way, everyone in the shop will be secretly imagining what you could do if you were *really* trying...

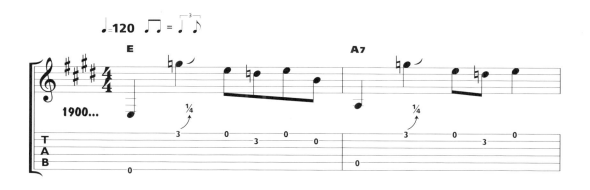

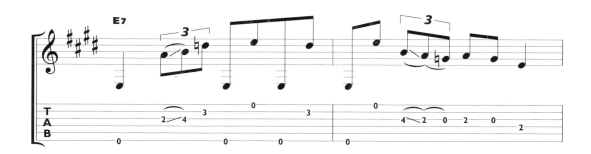

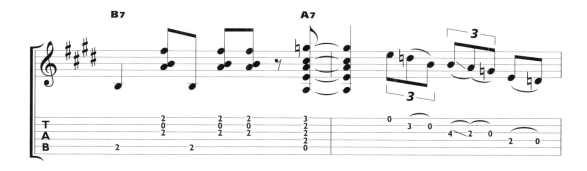

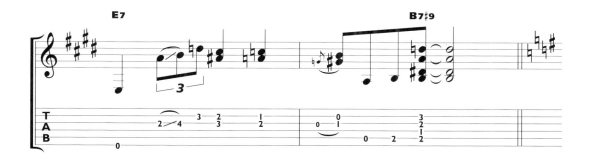

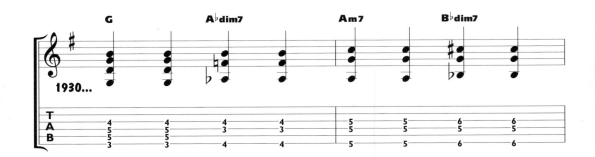

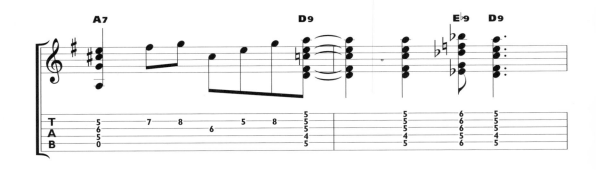

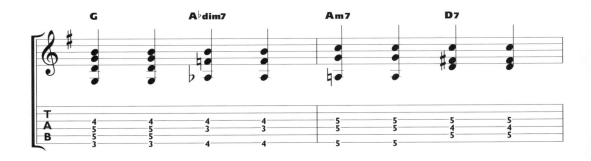

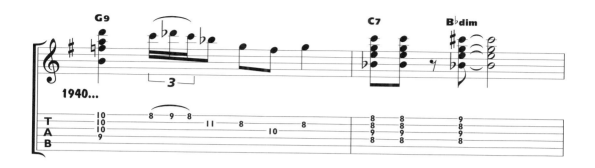

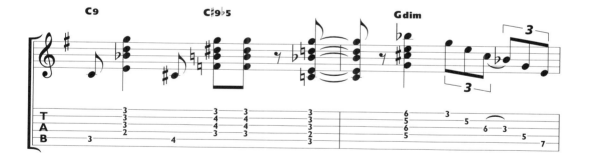

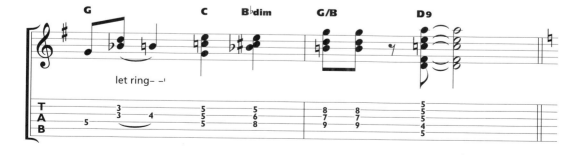

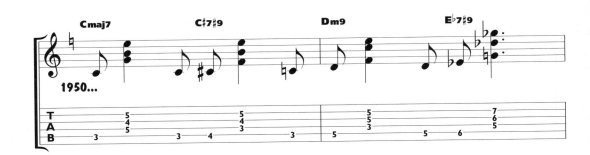

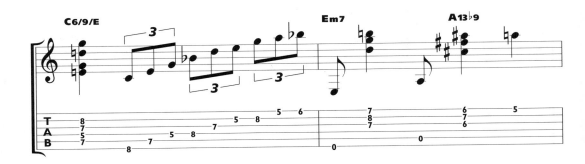

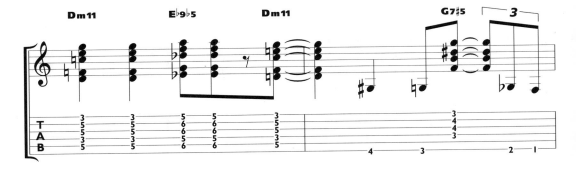

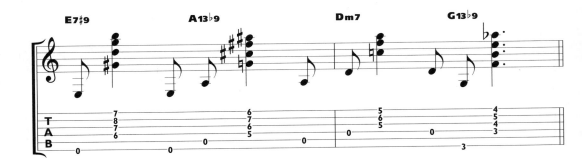

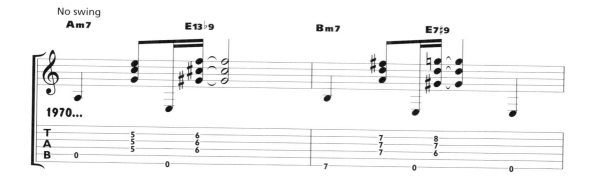

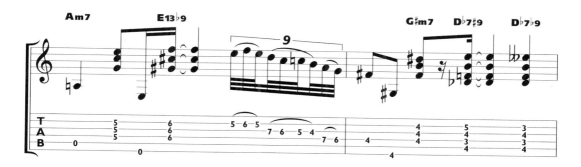

# Outro

So now you've got it all - the background information, the CD collection, the licks, the techniques and the theory. Only one thing remains – the etiquette. I'll leave you with a list of the dos and don'ts of playing in a live jazz band.

These rules have developed over generations, so break them at your own risk.

# Jazz Gig Etiquette

# Always...

**1** ...make sure you're *slightly* late for any rehearsal or gig. This will encourage other players to think of you as an eccentric genius rather than an unreliable loser. Probably. Hey, it worked for **Django**.

**2** ...nod your head appreciatively whilst someone else takes a solo. If you can do it with your eyes closed while comping and you still don't fall over, so much the better.

**3** ...listen to the band's backing. The most common complaint other players have with us guitarists is that we can't stay in time.

**4** ...use the oldest guitar you own. Pointy-headed Skull-fronted Death-Metal axes do not go down well with traditionalists.

**5** ...stand near the back of the band. Brass players hate to be upstaged.

**6** ...carry a tuner with you, and set it so you can tune up silently. Only prima donna sax players are allowed to tune up in front of an audience.

**7** ...cover your mistakes by repeating them several times over the following bars.

**8** ...quote **Charlie Parker**'s sax lines in your solos where possible. It's a real winner for those in the know.

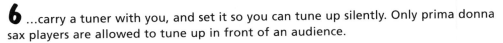

**9** ...admit when you've stolen a lick from a famous player. This will actually earn you respect.

**10** ...compliment other players on their 'nice chops' after hearing them blow over some changes.

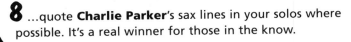

# Never...

**1** ...carry anyone else's gear. Even though the opposite is true in Rock and Blues gigs, just touching the beloved sax case/music stand/ gig bag is cause for justifiable homicide with some jazzers.

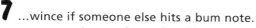

**2** ...look at your watch during someone else's solo.

**3** ...take a solo for more than 3 cycles of a standard unless you've had encouragement from the band leader.

**4** ...use a guitar synth to simulate brass sounds. It's not big and it certainly isn't clever.

**5** ...criticise **Django**.

**6** ...try to play a standard in a new band without a chart. Everyone will have a different idea of exactly what the changes are.

**7** ...wince if someone else hits a bum note. Just nod your head harder as if you've understood their harmonic dissonance, even if the audience hasn't.

**8** ...move the same barre chord shape up and down the neck. It's a dead giveaway that you're a rock player in disguise.

**9** ...pass off a famous player's lick as your own. If someone spots it, you're stuffed. You can just about get away with something like "it's a little **Montgomery** idea that I messed with a little, man" but you're skating on thin ice.

**10** ...admit to owning this book. The idea that you can "Bluff your way" in Jazz guitar is sacrilege to most players.

# And finally...

Always find out what the Bread (fee) is going to be *Before The Gig*. Any bandleader who says "We'll sort something out" – won't!

**Happy Bluffing!**

If you've enjoyed this book, why not check out the other books in this great new series, available from all good music and book retailers, or in case of difficulty, direct from Music Sales (see page 2).

# It's Easy To Bluff...

| Blues Guitar | Rock Guitar | Metal Guitar | Acoustic Guitar | Music Theory |
|---|---|---|---|---|
| AM955196 | AM955218 | AM955207 | AM955174 | AM958485 |

**JOE BENNETT** has been teaching guitar for fifteen years, and regularly works as a session guitarist. He is also a senior examiner in electric guitar for The London College of Music and Head of Popular Music at City of Bath College. Joe's publications include the *Guitar: To Go!* and *Really Easy Guitar* series, and *The Little Book of Scales*, plus tracks and articles for *Future Music*, *PowerOn* and *Total Guitar* magazines.